Martin Luther King Jr.

These and other titles are included in The Importance Of
biography series:

Alexander the Great	Harry Houdini
Muhammad Ali	Thomas Jefferson
Louis Armstrong	Mother Jones
James Baldwin	Chief Joseph
Clara Barton	John F. Kennedy
The Beatles	Martin Luther King Jr.
Napoleon Bonaparte	Joe Louis
Julius Caesar	Malcolm X
Rachel Carson	Thurgood Marshall
Charlie Chaplin	Margaret Mead
Charlemagne	Golda Meir
Cesar Chavez	Michelangelo
Winston Churchill	Wolfgang Amadeus Mozart
Cleopatra	John Muir
Christopher Columbus	Sir Isaac Newton
Hernando Cortes	Richard M. Nixon
Marie Curie	Georgia O'Keeffe
Charles Dickens	Louis Pasteur
Emily Dickinson	Pablo Picasso
Amelia Earhart	Elvis Presley
Thomas Edison	Jackie Robinson
Albert Einstein	Norman Rockwell
Duke Ellington	Eleanor Roosevelt
Dian Fossey	Anwar Sadat
Anne Frank	Margaret Sanger
Benjamin Franklin	Oskar Schindler
Galileo Galilei	William Shakespeare
Emma Goldman	John Steinbeck
Jane Goodall	Tecumseh
Martha Graham	Jim Thorpe
Lorraine Hansberry	Mark Twain
Stephen Hawking	Queen Victoria
Ernest Hemingway	Pancho Villa
Jim Henson	H. G. Wells
Adolf Hitler	

THE *IMPORTANCE OF*

Martin Luther King Jr.

by John F. Wukovits

Lucent Books, P.O. Box 289011, San Diego, CA 92198-9011

Library of Congress Cataloging-in-Publication Data

Wukovits, John F., 1944–
    Martin Luther King Jr. / by John F. Wukovits.
        p.   cm.—(The importance of)
    Includes bibliographical references and index.
    Summary: Discusses the childhood, education, social ac-
tivism, and assassination of the noted civil rights leader.
    ISBN 1–56006–483–8 (alk. paper)
    1. King, Martin Luther, Jr., 1929–1968—Juvenile literature.
2. Afro-Americans—Biography—Juvenile literature.   3. Civil
rights workers—United States—Biography—Juvenile literature. 4. Baptists—United States—Clergy—Biography—
Juvenile literature.   5. Afro-Americans—Civil rights—
History—20th century—Juvenile literature.   [1. King,
Martin Luther, Jr., 1929–1968.   2. Civil rights workers.
3. Clergy.   4. Afro-Americans—Biography.]   1. Title.
II. Series.
E185.97.K5W85   1999
323'.092—dc21   98–36197
    [B]   CIP
                                                      AC

Copyright 1999 by Lucent Books, Inc., P.O. Box 289011,
San Diego, California 92198-9011

Printed in the U.S.A.

Contents

A Fighter till the End

Stretching back to his earliest memories as a youth in Atlanta, Georgia, Martin Luther King Jr. lived with the destructive effects of a segregated society. He recalled the moment when he first realized that some people considered him inferior on account of the color of his skin. At age six, he romped through the neighborhood and played in backyards with his two closest friends, white boys whose father owned a nearby grocery store. They laughed and ran and shouted like other youngsters and eagerly looked forward to their next escapade.

Then one day it suddenly stopped. In September 1935, shortly before he and his friends were to enter school for the first time, King knocked on his friends' door. Instead of his playing companions, however, the parents answered and told Martin that their sons, who would attend the all-white neighborhood school while Martin attended an all-black school, could no longer play with him. As King remembered, "They weren't hostile; they just made excuses."[1] Because of his skin color, Martin was excluded from the normal childhood activity of playing with his friends.

Confused by this cold reaction, the youthful King rushed home, injured for the first time by bigotry's bitter sting.

Though often threatened with death, Martin Luther King Jr. never shrank from what he saw as his responsibility to denounce racism and violence. He urged his followers to maintain dignity and calm in the face of adversity.

Before this moment he felt just like his friends, acted like them, laughed and cried like them. Yet now he was told that, because of the color of his skin, he was not as good as someone else, that he had less worth simply because of his birth.

He walked through the doorway and asked his mother why white people hated black people. As King later wrote, "Every parent at some time faces the problem of explaining the facts of life to his child. Just as inevitably, for the Negro parent, the moment comes when he must explain to his offspring the facts of segregation."[2]

Alberta King, his mother, instinctively knew the hurt and doubts besieging her son and attempted to prepare him for the world he would face. She explained the history of black people in America—the slave trade, slave rebellions, the Civil War, prominent black leaders, the bigotry and segregation. After parading an array of people and events before his eyes, Alberta added "the words that almost every Negro hears before he can yet understand the injustice that makes them necessary: 'You are as good as anyone.'"[3] She emphasized that Martin must never feel inferior to anyone and must remember that he possessed dignity in equal measure with all other children.

The Early Fighter

Shunned by the white majority because he was black, King nevertheless matured into one of the most eloquent opponents of bigotry. Earning excellent marks at each step of his educational process and heavily influenced by history's great philosophers and theologians, King chose to follow in his father's footsteps and become a Baptist minis-ter. From the pulpit, King first used the power of words to draw attention to society's ills. As a youth he had boasted to his parents, "You just wait and see. When I grow up I'm going to get me some big words."[4]

Within a few months after accepting his first pastorship—the Dexter Avenue Baptist Church in Montgomery, Alabama—events swept King to the forefront of the civil rights movement. Now, rather than fighting solely from the pulpit, King's arena widened to the American South.

King faced imprisonment, death threats, and violence, yet he refused to shrink from what he saw as his responsibility. He urged his followers to avoid responding to violence with still more violence.

Mahatma Gandhi (pictured) inspired Martin Luther King's use of peaceful nonviolence in his fight against racial injustice.

Instead, he explained, in the mode of Jesus Christ and Indian leader Mahatma Gandhi, let peaceful nonviolence be the answer. If a bigot hurls an insult at you, do not answer. If a hate-filled individual throws rocks your way or rushes forward with a club, maintain dignity and calm.

King illustrated this approach in Mississippi with a handful of murderers standing directly behind him. Marching into Neshoba County, where three civil rights workers had been brutally slain, King and his close friend Ralph Abernathy stepped toward a courthouse to lead a group in prayer for equality. King glanced toward the angry white mob gathering behind them, knowing that the murderers of the three workers most likely stood within the group. He thought that he was about to die. As he dropped to his knees to pray, he muttered to a hostile Mississippi sheriff, "I believe the murderers are somewhere around me at this moment." The law officer, who had sworn to uphold the law but instead allowed Mississippi blacks to be terrorized, replied, "You damn right. They're right behind you."[5] King and Abernathy, though surrounded by people who wanted them dead, completed their prayer, rose, and calmly left the courthouse steps.

Besieged on All Sides

King's battleground stretched across the entire nation, for bigotry and prejudice had wound their destructive tentacles about much of American society. Years of mistreatment in the South produced a system that kept blacks in an inferior position. Held down by Jim Crow laws, blacks could not attend the mainstream public

Martin Luther King Jr. (right) and Reverend Ralph Abernathy led the black bus boycott in Montgomery, Alabama.

school system, could not vote, could not ride in the front seats of buses, and could not exercise many rights guaranteed to citizens by the nation's Constitution.

While King battled these abuses, he faced the open opposition of numerous local, state, and federal government officials who believed, at a minimum, that King fomented more harm with his campaigns. Thus, he not only fought to change an evil system, but he also battled with elected men who were determined to uphold that system. Local sheriffs and police officers quickly resorted to cracking skulls and arresting civil rights marchers, while national politicians issued pronouncements that opposed King's tactics.

Jim Crow Laws

Jim Crow laws—statutes designed to keep black people in a subservient state—existed for decades after the Civil War supposedly ended slavery. Historian John Hope Franklin explains their origin in his book From Slavery to Freedom: A History of Negro Americans.

"Beginning in Tennessee in 1870, Southerners enacted laws against intermarriage of the races in every Southern state. Five years later, Tennessee adopted the first 'Jim Crow' law, and the rest of the South rapidly fell in line. Negroes and whites were separated on trains, in depots, and on wharves. After the Supreme Court in 1883 outlawed the Civil Rights Acts of 1875, the Negro was banned from white hotels, barber shops, restaurants, and theaters. By 1885 most Southern states had laws requiring separate schools."

The racist laws of the southern states forced black men and women into separate, and often inferior, facilities.

Most detrimental to King in this area was the reaction of the head of the Federal Bureau of Investigation (FBI), J. Edgar Hoover. An intolerant, narrow-minded individual who imagined a Communist conspiracy in most everything he disliked, Hoover ordered FBI agents to closely monitor King's movements and telephone conversations. Through legal and illegal methods, the FBI compiled an immense file on King and even used its contents to threaten the civil rights leader.

Perhaps most perplexing to King, though, was apathy. Too many citizens had grown accustomed to the way things were and saw little reason to change. As long as their world drifted along in relative peace and quiet, they tended to ignore calls from people like King who proposed radical alterations. King battled every day to reach the "average" American and show that, while the country could boast of many achievements for which all could be proud, it still had a distance to travel to achieve equal rights for blacks.

As if opposition from much of the nation was not enough, King also received criticism from within the black community. Some blacks viewed King as a threat to their position in the business world or in society; others considered King's calls for social justice as nothing more than a rationale for the forces of southern bigotry to unleash worse indignities upon oppressed southern blacks. Simultaneously, black radicals and revolutionaries thought that King's civil rights activities did not go far enough to achieve true change. They labeled King an "Uncle Tom," a black who worked with the white majority to maintain the status quo. Often King believed that no matter what he did, someone waited to heap heavy criticism on him.

He could turn to his family for comfort, and often did, but even here he waged a war between family responsibility and his civil rights commitments. While he yearned for the time when he could romp about the yard with his children or leisurely travel with his wife, King never could escape the crushing duties imposed by his civil rights work. Frequent absences from his family bothered King, yet he could not turn his back upon such historic work.

King also struggled with a personal demon—while he dearly loved his wife, he did not stay faithful to her while he was on the road. Although these infidelities filled him with enormous guilt, he aggravated his situation by continued transgressions; he knew he was wrong and attempted to stop. As he stated in a sermon, "Each of us is two selves. And the great burden of life is to always try to keep that higher self in command. Don't let the lower self take over."[6]

King's Importance

Martin Luther King Jr. contributed to American history as few people have. His speeches moved people not only to tears but, more importantly, to action. His words unlocked the shackles that had constrained an entire group and gave hope to the downtrodden that a better future awaited. Through his activities, King placed dignity in calloused, scarred hands that had rarely, if ever, known such a quality. His deeds imparted the noble feeling that average Americans could work to solve society's ills.

A prominent civil rights worker of the past thirty years, Julian Bond, summarizes King's importance:

He made popular the idea that individuals are capable of changing their situation. Through the protests of the 1960s, it was demonstrated that black people could do this, and now you see larger groups of people doing it. Women, farmers and others have seized upon nonviolent protest as a means of advancing their cause. Although Martin Luther King didn't invent sit-in demonstrations and didn't invent mass marches, he made them available to the larger body of the American population.

As one of King's closest friends, Andrew Young, mentions, "I think his important legacy is that human problems, no matter how big, can be solved."[7]

1 "The Curtain Had Dropped on My Selfhood"

Born in 1897 on a rural farm in central Georgia to poor parents, Martin's father, Michael "Daddy" King, experienced segregation on a daily basis. He witnessed whites beating blacks for the slightest reasons and once saw a neighbor lynched.

In 1915 Michael King decided that he would never amount to much if he remained on the farm, so he headed for Atlanta with ambitions of becoming a Baptist minister. After working during the day and attending night classes to receive a high school diploma, in 1926 Michael entered Morehouse College, a prominent black institution. That same year he married Alberta Williams, the daughter of the Baptist pastor of one of Atlanta's leading black churches, the Ebenezer Baptist Church. The happy couple shared a home with Alberta's parents, moving into the top floor of a twelve-room home at 501 Auburn Avenue, a respectable black neighborhood. Michael was named assistant pastor at the church, and rose to pastor in 1931 when Reverend Williams died.

King's Childhood

Within a few years Michael King and his wife gave birth to three children: a daughter in 1927, named Willie Christine, and two boys, Michael Jr., born January 15, 1929, in a bedroom of the Auburn Avenue home, and Alfred Daniel, or A. D., born in 1930. Five years later, to recognize his own increasing importance in Atlanta's religious community, Daddy changed both his name and his first son's to Martin Luther King Sr. and Jr. in honor of the founder of the Lutheran religion.

According to Martin Luther King Jr., called M. L., the family lived comfortably.

Martin Luther King Sr. and his wife Alberta instilled in their son the belief that the injustice perpetrated on them by southern whites should be opposed.

His father earned enough money to provide whatever they needed, and there was certainly sufficient room in the large house for three young children and two grandparents. King later wrote that they never lived in a rented house or owed money on a car.

Family and religion loomed large in King's youth. His father, the family disciplinarian, expected his children to obey him, and he did not shy from administering a whipping should any of the three act up. Since the energetic Martin always seemed to be flirting with trouble, Daddy had to apply more than a fair share of punishment to his middle child.

While he loved his father and mother, whom he and his siblings called "Mother Dear," young Martin formed the closest bond with his grandmother. Affectionately called "Mama," Grandmother Williams provided love and tenderness to each of the three children, particularly after a spanking. Little Martin sought her out following a punishment, knowing that she would soothe his feelings with tender words and gentle hugs. King later recalled that "She was very dear to each of us, but especially to me."[8]

M. L. lived as normal a life as any black youth could in the Deep South. He worked odd jobs around the neighborhood to earn spending money and, at the age of eight, delivered newspapers for the Atlanta *Journal.* He performed so well in the latter job that five years later he was promoted to assistant manager for one of the business's delivery stations, thereby becoming the youngest to fill such a responsible post.

M. L. loved most sports, and though small compared with the other boys, he participated with an intensity few could match. He detested losing and would do

Though not initially inclined toward the ministry, King eventually followed his father to the pulpit.

almost anything to win. On the basketball court King wanted the ball in his hands so he could shoot, and he always claimed the fullback position in football in which, as one friend explained, "he ran over anybody who got in his way."[9] Rarely a contest ended without King instigating a fight with one of the other players.

A direct contrast to the leisurely activities was the family's emphasis on religion. None of the children knew when Daddy might ask them to recite biblical passages at dinner, and M. L. spent hours every Sunday in the Ebenezer Baptist Church listening to his father's sermons or attending funerals and weddings.

Though some boys might have rebelled at spending Sundays in this manner, King did not object. He loved reading—rarely was he without a book—and his

The white waiting area at a bus depot in the South. When King was a high school student, he and his teacher were forced to give up their seats to white passengers while returning from a speaking contest in Dublin, Georgia. They had to stand for the ninety-mile trip to Atlanta.

father's sermons captivated him. As a result he developed an extensive vocabulary at an early age and peppered his parents and other adults with questions about different subjects. King displayed an incredible talent for memorizing lengthy poems and could sing from memory just about any song in the hymnal.

Encounters with Segregation

In many ways Martin experienced a typical life for a youth of his day. The one glaring exception—and it made all the difference—was that he grew up black in a southern society that handed all the advantages to

King and His Grandmother

Martin Luther King Jr. developed a deep affection for his grandmother. In his account of King, Parting the Waters: America in the King Years, 1954–1963, *Taylor Branch recalls a childhood incident.*

"A. D. [King's brother] once slid down a bannister at high speed into grandmother Williams, knocking her into a heap on the floor. As her relatives raced to her from all points in the house, and were shouting and moaning and wondering how to tell whether she was alive, a far deeper panic seized M. L. He ran upstairs to his room at the back of the house and threw himself out the window. A new round of cries from the children brought horror to the elder Kings, when, just as Mrs. Williams was beginning to revive, they had to run outside to their older son, who did not move until he heard that his grandmother was alive."

whites. Society, according to King, dished out daily reminders that he occupied an inferior status to whites.

King could not walk into an Atlanta drugstore and order a soda or sandwich as did white boys and girls. If he was thirsty or had to use a rest room when in town, laws prohibited him from using the modern drinking fountains and clean rest rooms bearing the sign For Whites Only. Instead, he had to skirt around to the "colored" fountains and filthy "colored" rest rooms. If he needed to travel any distance and had to use the city's bus system, southern society forced him to sit in the back of the bus so that whites could sit in the front, and he understood that no matter what the black male's age, whites called him "boy." King could not cool off from the summer's heat by jumping in a city swimming pool, for those were reserved For Whites Only, and despite the fact that he lived in a large, comfortable house, King knew that whites called his section of Atlanta "nigger town."

King heard the stories of angry white mobs apprehending innocent blacks throughout the South and lynching them. So many blacks had been hanged in the South—more than three thousand in eighty years—that the famous American writer Mark Twain sarcastically labeled the

A mob gathers to witness a lynching. Since the end of the Civil War, more than three thousand blacks were lynched by angry white mobs in the South.

nation "the United States of Lyncherdom." It did not matter that King had never seen a lynching, as had his father, or even a vicious beating; stories about such incidents were sufficient to do the harm. Noted black author Richard Wright, who was born in Lousiana, remembers that

> the things that influenced my conduct as a Negro did not have to happen to me directly; I needed but to hear of them to feel their full effects in the deepest layers of my consciousness. Indeed, the white brutality that I had not seen was a more effective control of my behavior than that which I knew.[10]

If one doubted that violence could strike at any moment, the eight-year-old Martin observed a shocking reminder when members of the Ku Klux Klan, a hate group devoted to promoting whites and subjugating blacks, marched straight down Auburn Avenue—Martin's street—in a grand parade.

The Ku Klux Klan was a huge presence in Martin Luther King Jr.'s neighborhood. In 1936 they paraded down an Atlanta street just blocks from his home.

King Could Fight or Talk

Martin Luther King Jr. eventually became known as an apostle for nonviolence, but as Stephen Oates explains in his biography Let the Trumpet Sound, *in his youth King showed that he would resort to fighting if need be.*

"He also had his share of fights, excelling in what an associate termed 'middle-class combat.' He never battled with knives and stones, as lower-class boys often did. And he preferred negotiation to fisticuffs. But if negotiation failed, M. L.'s ritual remark was 'let's go to the grass,' and he tore into his adversary. 'He could outwrestle anybody in our gang,' a chum said, 'and he knew it.' In all, young King was 'a bit of a hellion' and subject to 'violent swings in mood.'"

A black youth who garnered headlines for her courageous actions as a member of the first nine black students to enroll in Central High School in Little Rock, Arkansas, Melba Pattillo Beals, writes of growing up in the South during the 1940s:

> Black folks aren't born expecting segregation, prepared from day one to follow its confining rules. Nobody presents you with a handbook when you're teething and says, "Here's how you must behave as a second-class citizen." Instead, the humiliating expectations and traditions of segregation creep over you, slowly stealing a teaspoonful of your self-esteem each day.[11]

Southern society tried in every way to strip blacks of their dignity. One day while King shopped in a downtown department store, a white woman slapped him and called him a "little nigger" because he had accidentally stepped in her way. On another occasion he purchased a ticket to an Atlanta movie theater only to be humiliated by the requirement that he sit far in the back balcony with the other black children. "The experience of having to enter a rear door and sit in a filthy peanut gallery was so obnoxious that I could not enjoy the picture." For similar reasons he despised the separate restaurants and other facilities, "partly because the separate was always unequal, and partly because the very idea of separation did something to my sense of dignity and self-respect."[12]

Daddy King's Example

Whenever King's parents advised him to love whites in spite of their actions, he wondered, "How can I love a race of people who hate me?" Instead, he reacted with bitterness to his earliest episodes of segregation and recalled that "from that moment on I was determined to hate every white person."[13]

The colored entrance to a movie theater in the South. As a child, King was constantly exposed to the fact that he and other blacks were considered to be second-class citizens. Segregation was a tool used to enforce that inferiority.

On the other hand, King had the example of his father to counter segregation's negative force. Proud of his heritage and even prouder of his accomplishments, Daddy King bowed to no one. He combined love of fellow man with insistence that he be treated with at least a semblance of respect by white society. He may not be accorded equality, but he would maintain his dignity. The son carefully watched his father, and from him he began learning that hate was not the answer.

One day father and son entered a downtown shoe store and sat in seats near the store's front. A young white clerk mentioned that he would wait on them "if you'll just move to those seats in the rear." When Daddy replied, "There's nothing wrong with these seats. We're quite comfortable here," the clerk repeated that they would have to move. Daddy stated with polite firmness, "We'll either buy shoes sitting here, or we won't buy shoes at all." Reaching over to take his son's hand, Daddy then rose and walked out of the store, without shoes but with his dignity intact. The son recalled years later that "This was the first time I had ever seen my father so angry. I still remember walking down the street beside him as he muttered, 'I don't care how long I have to live with this system, I will never accept it.'" [14]

Another time King and his father were riding in their car when a police officer pulled them over for speeding. "All right, boy," barked the officer to Daddy King, "pull over and let me see your license." Restraining his anger but with emotion seeping through clenched teeth, Daddy replied, "I'm no boy." He pointed to his son and added, "This is a boy. I'm a man, and until you call me one, I will not listen to you." [15] Words like these could fre-

quently result in a speedy arrest or beating, but the policeman was so stunned by the force of Daddy's words that he simply wrote the ticket and left.

Martin learned as much about how to deal with being black in a segregated society from his father's actions as he did listening to his words. Daddy made sure he emphasized certain points to his son, such as his assertion that "When I stand up, I want everybody to know that a *man* is standing," or that "Nobody can make a slave out of you if you don't think like a slave." [16] However, he made a stronger impact by following up his words with action.

Martin observed this in the shoe store and with the police officer, and he saw it reinforced in numerous other instances. When Daddy learned that some of Atlanta's blacks received harsh treatment by the city's bus drivers, he refused to use that method of transportation. He helped gain improved wages for black schoolteachers in town and led a successful campaign to eliminate the use of segregated elevators in the courthouse. Because of his work Daddy earned the respect of Atlanta's black population and even the grudging admiration of some moderate white citizens. As a result, Martin learned that insistence upon respect, combined with a willingness to battle for one's beliefs, could achieve far more than the hatred he earlier felt.

Elementary and High School

King advanced with ease through elementary school and high school, always accumulating top grades. In January 1942, when King was in eighth grade, school officials at the Atlanta University Laboratory

King Learns His Heritage

Like all blacks growing up in the South of the 1940s, King quickly experienced discrimination and abuse. However, he used it to his advantage rather than let it blind him to goodness and decency. Flip Schulke and Penelope McPhee relate one such incident in their book King Remembered.

"But even the most loving assurances of a mother and grandmother could not protect an unsuspecting child from the surprise attacks of white prejudice. Once, while Martin stood in front of an Atlanta store waiting for his mother, a total stranger slapped him across the face. 'That little nigger stepped on my foot,' the woman said to a bystander.

Endeavoring to understand this kind of cruelty and humiliation, M. L. began to read avidly about the history of his people, about slavery and the Civil War, about such black men as Frederick Douglass, Nat Turner, Denmark Vesey, and Booker T. Washington. 'He read everything he could on these things,' said his father. 'He was making preparations.'"

Booker T. Washington (pictured) and other black people who figured prominently in American history inspired Martin Luther King Jr. to fight bigotry and hate.

School moved him up to the ninth grade because he had performed so well. After only six months in the ninth grade, King entered tenth grade in the fall of 1942 at the Booker T. Washington High School.

The well-mannered King was one of the school's most popular students. Not only did he earn high marks in class, but the girls flocked around him, drawn by his impeccable style of clothing, his deep, pleasant voice, and his agility on the dance floor, where he loved to jitterbug the night away. King, teasingly called "Tweed" by the boys because he loved to wear a brown tweed suit with baggy trousers, rarely lacked a date for any occasion. King claimed that in those years, his two main weaknesses were women and food.

Two incidents during his high school years left their mark on King. In his junior year, the fourteen-year-old King entered a speaking contest sponsored by a black organization. He and his teacher, Mrs. Bradley, traveled ninety miles to Dublin, Georgia, where King delivered a speech titled "The Negro and the Constitution." He so moved the judges with his oration that they awarded King first prize.

The jubilant pair boarded the bus for the lengthy ride home and passed the time reminiscing about the happy event. Their laughter and joy quickly melted to humiliation and anger, however, when the bus pulled into a small town along the route. A group of white passengers entered the crowded bus; to make room for the additional people, the bus driver turned to King and Mrs. Bradley. As was legal in those days, he ordered them to leave their seats and move to the back so the whites could sit near the front. King recalls the incident:

> We didn't move quickly enough to suit him, so he began cursing us, calling us "black sons of bitches." I intended to stay right in that seat, but Mrs. Bradley finally urged me up, saying we had to obey the law. And so we stood up in the aisle for the ninety miles to Atlanta. That night will never leave my memory. It was the angriest I have ever been in my life.[17]

First Taste of Freedom

After obtaining early admission to Morehouse College in early 1944, King embarked on his first visit outside the South. He spent the summer working on a Connecticut farm, and for the first time he experienced a freedom that southern society would not permit. In Connecticut, King could eat wherever he chose, could walk anywhere in public parks, and could sit in the front rows of movie theaters. He did not have to worry about offending a passing white citizen or about having to yield his seat to anyone else. Connecticut was a breath of fresh air for King, who loved "the exhilarating sense of freedom"[18] offered during that summer.

Harsh reality returned on his train ride back to Atlanta. While the train traveled in northern states, King could sit anywhere and was free to move about, but when it pulled into Virginia, conditions quickly changed. When King entered the dining car, instead of seating him at a main table, the waiter guided King to a rear table and pulled a curtain so that white passengers would not have to see a black in the same room. King, in no mood to eat, stared in dismay at the curtain as the train lumbered deeper into the South and segregation. "I felt as though the curtain had dropped on my selfhood,"[19] King later wrote.

2 "A Moral Obligation to Return"

King headed into his college years with different thoughts for his future than his father, who hoped his son would enter the ministry and join him at Ebenezer Baptist. King was uncomfortable with the emotionalism of Negro religion and preferred what he considered a more rational approach based on knowledge and learning.

He looked forward to completing his college education, attaining an advanced degree, and then delving into the academic world as a professor of theology or philosophy. At the age of fifteen, after being advanced ahead of his class due to superior grades, King first walked into university life in September 1944 by enrolling at Atlanta's prestigious Morehouse College, considered by many to be "the black Harvard."

Morehouse College

Morehouse opened King's mind to exciting possibilities. A string of illustrious professors introduced him to the world's great thinkers and challenged King to analyze his goals. The college president, an active civil rights leader named Dr. Benjamin Mays, used the pulpit to calmly espouse his belief that one not only must be religious but also must take a vibrant role in changing society for the better. This message struck a nerve with King, who scribbled pages of notes as Mays delivered each sermon. For the first time, King watched in action a minister who fit the mold of what he believed a modern minister must be—someone who relied on reason to convey his message and who was willing to enter the fight for social justice.

His sociology professor, Walter Chivers, reinforced the notion of social activism. According to one of King's close friends at Morehouse, Walter McCall, Chivers "constantly brought before us the serious social problems of the day. Particularly, we discussed very seriously at many times the role of leadership in liberating the Negro."[20]

Professor George Kelsey taught King that, while he might dismiss certain biblical accounts as legends or tales, he must not ignore the truths that those stories related. In that manner, Kelsey taught that a minister could use the messages of the Bible to advance social reform. In another class, King read Henry David Thoreau's essay "Civil Disobedience" and realized that passive, nonviolent resistance could be a powerful tool for change.

Morehouse's professors challenged King to find solutions to social issues, instead of simply complaining about them.

Henry David Thoreau (pictured) championed his views of passive, nonviolent resistance in his essay "Civil Disobedience." His opinions significantly influenced King's strategy for fighting racism.

individuals were better than others because of skin color, were the problem. When he joined the Atlanta Intercollegiate Council, an interracial student group, King solidified his views. "As I got to see more of white people, my resentment softened and a spirit of cooperation took its place."[21]

Convinced that one could thus fight to improve society while remaining in the ministry, in 1947 King announced his intention to become a minister. His ecstatic father quickly scheduled a sermon for his son to deliver at Ebenezer, and afterward Daddy boasted that his talented son would one day make a fine preacher. In February 1948 King was ordained and joined his father as assistant pastor at Ebenezer. Four months later he received a bachelor of arts degree in sociology from Morehouse.

Crozer Theological Seminary

King often stayed up much of the night discussing these points with classmates and searching for answers to society's ills, particularly those dealing with segregation. As a result, King took his first active step by writing a letter to the Atlanta *Constitution* stating that blacks were entitled to the same rights as any other American citizen, a bold proposal to submit to a southern newspaper. He quit one summer job when a white foreman called him a nigger, and at another summer job he noticed that black workers received less pay than white workers, even though they performed the same duties.

He also realized, however, that whites as a group were not the problem. People filled with hate, who boasted that certain

Following graduation from Morehouse, King entered Crozer Theological Seminary, an integrated school of one hundred students in Chester, Pennsylvania, to gain a master's degree in philosophy. Not only was King among white students for the first time, but he was also outside of his father's reach. At Crozer, King could form his personal beliefs and guiding philosophy without worrying about the strong influence of Daddy King.

As one of the six blacks among the student population, King intended to dispel any false notions his white counterparts may have had:

I was well aware of the typical white stereotype of the Negro, that he is always late, that he's loud and always laughing, that he's dirty and messy, and for a while I was terribly conscious of trying to avoid identification with it. If I were a minute late to class, I was almost morbidly conscious of it and sure that everyone else noticed it. Rather than be thought of as always laughing, I'm afraid I was grimly serious at the time. I had a tendency to overdress, to keep my room spotless, my shoes perfectly shined and my clothes immaculately pressed.[22]

Crozer continued expanding the outlook that King had begun formulating at Morehouse. Receiving A's in every course, King read the works of great philosophers such as Plato, Aristotle, Jean-Jacques Rousseau, Georg Hegel, and Immanuel Kant. He absorbed Karl Marx's *Communist Manifesto* but dismissed it as immoral. He was moved by the American theologian Reinhold Niebuhr, who advocated activism, and by Walter Rauschenbusch's "Social Gospel," which encouraged people to become involved in changing society. King was more convinced than ever that religion and ministers had to be concerned with more than a person's soul. As he writes, "any religion which professes to be concerned about the souls of men and is not concerned about the social and economic conditions that scar the soul is a spiritually moribund religion."[23]

Following Gandhi's Lead

One particular Sunday, King attended a lecture by the president of Howard University, Dr. Mordecai W. Johnson. The lecture changed King's life. Johnson spoke of his recent visit to India, where the Indian leader Mahatma Gandhi had recently won independence from Great Britain for his nation by relying on nonviolent resistance such as boycotts, strikes, and marches. King soaked in each word, then hastened to a bookstore and purchased an armful of books on Gandhi. He had found his

King's Speaking Skills

In his history of the civil rights movement, Parting the Waters: America in the King Years, 1954–1963, *Taylor Branch speaks of King's oratorical skills.*

"King's oratory was among his chief distinctions at Crozer [Seminary]. His peers so admired his preaching technique that they packed the chapel whenever he delivered the regular Thursday student sermon, and kibitzers drifted into practice preaching classes when King was at the podium. A generation later, some of the white students who remembered very little else about King would remember the text, theme, and impact of specific King practice sermons."

role model in the diminutive Indian leader, and the more he read about the man, the more determined King was that nonviolence would be the way to change American society. King now had a method to go along with his philosophy of social activism.

Daily events reminded King that change was needed. In June 1950 he and three companions drove to a restaurant in New Jersey. When the waitress ignored them, King stated that discrimination was illegal in the state and asked to see the owner. Brandishing a pistol, the owner barged out and shouted that if they did not leave, he would shoot. As the four turned and walked out, the owner fired a few shots over their heads for effect. Though King filed a complaint with the police, the case was dropped when no witnesses came forward to support King.

In another incident a white student from North Carolina banged on King's door, claiming that King had messed up his room. Though another student had pulled the prank, the white classmate pulled out a pistol and threatened to shoot King if he did not admit his guilt. King calmly stared back at his adversary and asserted that he had done nothing; and before the gun-wielding student could do anything, onlookers rushed in and separated the two.

Though King could have pressed charges, he declined. In response to bitter criticism from other white students, the North Carolina classmate publicly apologized to King, who became one of the campus's most popular students for the calm manner in which he handled the incident. Though King was stung by the student's hate, he also saw that nonviolence had defused a volatile situation, and he was heart-ened by the warm response of many other white students.

In May 1951 King received his bachelor of divinity degree from Crozer. Since he accumulated the highest grades in his class, King delivered a commencement speech as valedictorian, then received the faculty's Pearl Plafker Memorial Award as outstanding student and a twelve-hundred-dollar scholarship for graduate work.

King Meets Coretta Scott

King selected Boston University for his doctorate work. As he did at each step in his education, King compiled high marks. He loved spending hours reading, reflecting, and debating, and he planned that one day he would enjoy the happy life of a university professor. King did so well that his adviser ranked him among the top five students he had ever taught.

The handsome, intelligent King had no difficulty finding attractive females to date, yet in Boston he missed what he considered the grace and charm of a southern woman. When he mentioned that to a friend one day, she said that she knew a music student from Alabama who might be willing to go out. In February 1952 King called Coretta Scott and asked her for a date. She had heard of King and hesitated because she feared he might be a strict fundamentalist preacher, but he assured her he was not.

The two met over lunch the next day. Scott's confidence impressed King, while she was taken with his intelligence, sincerity, and eloquence. As King drove her home, he declared, "You have everything I have ever wanted in a wife. There are only four things, and you have them all." When

Mahatma Gandhi

The inspiration for much of King's work was the Indian leader Mahatma Gandhi, who relied on a nonviolent approach to achieve his goal of Indian independence from Great Britain. Jules Archer, in his book They Had a Dream: The Civil Rights Struggle, *points out Gandhi's influence.*

"Martin was excited by a lecture on the great Indian leader Mahatma Gandhi and his nonviolent resistance against political injustice. Buying books on Gandhi, Martin devoured them eagerly. An inspiration seized him. Why not combine the teachings of Gandhi, Thoreau, and Jesus Christ to combat unjust laws against blacks? Martin felt confident he could persuade blacks to break prejudicial laws, then allow themselves to be arrested and jailed as martyrs.

The secret weapon of blacks, he would preach, should be love instead of hate, transforming white hearts."

Mahatma Gandhi (seen here fourth from left with his followers in a peaceful protest march) inspired King to fight injustice not with hate but with love.

In February 1952, while working on his doctorate at Boston University, King met Coretta Scott. They were married on June 18, 1953.

she replied that he did not even know her, he quickly responded, "Yes, I can tell. The four things that I look for in a wife are character, intelligence, personality, and beauty. And you have them all."[24]

The two began dating and before long were engaged. Though Daddy King opposed their marriage and wanted his son to marry a girl from a respectable Atlanta family, King refused to buckle. With his father's reluctant blessings, the two were married on June 18, 1953, on the front lawn of Scott's parents' home in Marion, Alabama, with brother A. D. as best man. Since the South contained few bridal suites for blacks, the newlyweds spent their wedding night in the home of a friend who was an undertaker. King later loved to tease people by telling them, "Do you know we spent our honeymoon at a funeral parlor?"[25]

The couple returned to Boston to complete their studies. Since Coretta had a heavy class schedule, for the next year Martin cleaned the apartment, washed clothes, and cooked dinners.

His First Post—Dexter Avenue Baptist Church

They would not long remain in Boston. In January 1954 King met with a group of

action, and he set up a meeting with black religious and civic leaders for that night.

Friday evening King convened a meeting of fifty black ministers and community leaders. To King's dismay, the group reflected both the hopes and the fears of Montgomery's blacks. Some leaders advocated an unyielding boycott, arguing that the loss of bus revenue would cause the city's white establishment to cave in. Others cautioned that such an approach would only invite a violent reaction from bigots.

A Lifelong Feeling

In her autobiography, Rosa Parks: My Story, *Parks mentions the decades of abuse directed toward blacks that culminated with her refusal to leave her bus seat.*

"For half of my life there were laws and customs in the South that kept African Americans segregated from Caucasians and allowed white people to treat black people without any respect. I never thought this was fair, and from the time I was a child, I tried to protest against disrespectful treatment. But it was very hard to do anything about segregation and racism when white people had the power of the law behind them.

Somehow we had to change the laws."

Accompanied by her attorney, Rosa Parks is led to jail by a deputy in Montgomery, Alabama. She was arrested for not giving up her bus seat to a white person.

The gathering finally voted to boycott Montgomery's buses and set Monday, December 5, as the start. Each minister planned to inform his congregation on Sunday and organize groups of black citizens to pass out leaflets about the boycott. Representatives of black-owned taxi companies agreed to lower their prices to those charged by the buses so that blacks could get to work and travel about without undue hardship. Though pleased that his associates had united behind the move, King doubted that more than 60 percent of black riders would actually boycott Monday morning.

Since one of the city's busiest bus stops stood directly in front of his home, King got up early Monday to see how many riders boycotted the 6:00 A.M. bus. King was pouring a cup of coffee when his wife shouted for him to rush to the living room. He ran to the front door, where, to his delight and relief, he watched an empty bus drive up, stop, then pull away still empty.

King hurried to his car to check other bus stops around the city and found the same story unfolding at each location—the only blacks waiting were those singing, "No riders today." [31] Blacks used taxis or hitchhiked to school or work. Some walked twelve miles to reach their jobs, and one man even rode a mule. Montgomery's blacks, shoved around for so long, had pushed back as an organized unit for the first time. "A miracle had taken place," explained King. "The once dormant and quiescent Negro community was now fully awake." [32]

King's Powerful Speech

On Monday afternoon, after a court had found Parks guilty of violating a state segregation law and fined her fourteen dollars, black leaders formed the Montgomery Improvement Association (MIA) and selected King as its president. Though young, he was new to town and thus acceptable to the various factions. King demurred at taking the post and thought that a more experienced man should assume the obligation. However, Nixon

---

Copied Material?

Like every individual King suffered from shortcomings. Adam Fairclough writes of one in his biography Martin Luther King Jr.

"He moved through school and college with consummate ease—even if he did plagiarize large chunks of his Ph.D. dissertation. . . . The King Papers project, which is publishing King's collected writings and speeches under the direction of Clayborne Carson, has established beyond doubt that King's Ph.D. dissertation, and many of his graduate essays, contain numerous unattributed quotations from published sources."

An empty Montgomery city bus proves the effectiveness of the boycott. King at first had doubts about the number of blacks who would participate in the strike.

quickly quashed such talk. "You ain't got much time to think, 'cause you in the chair from now on."[33]

King's first step was to draft a speech he had to deliver that night at the Holt Street Baptist Church. Though he normally spent hours preparing each sermon, King had only twenty minutes to gather his thoughts before leaving for the church. The burden of the crushing responsibility almost overwhelmed the young minister, who knew that he had to find the correct words to arouse the people without inciting them to violence. He also realized that newspaper reporters would be in the crowd to record his speech.

By the time King stepped to the podium, people occupied every seat, stood in the aisles and hallways, and overflowed into the streets outside. After pausing a few seconds to gain everyone's attention, King explained the reasons for the boycott. As he slowly gained momentum, King's deep voice and ringing phrases captured the crowd and carried it along on an emotional ride.

King proclaimed that "there comes a time when people get tired. We are here this evening to say to those who have mistreated us so long that we are tired—tired of being segregated and humiliated; tired of being kicked about by the brutal feet of oppression." He mentioned that black citizens had been so patient over the years that white people believed they were actually happy with their subservient position. "But we come here tonight to be saved, to be saved from patience that makes us patient with anything less than freedom and justice."

True to his belief in nonviolence, King cautioned that "there will be no cross burnings. No white person will be taken from his home by a hooded Negro mob and brutally murdered. There will be no threats and intimidation. We must be guided by the highest principles of law and order." He urged that "love must be our regulating ideal" and that "we must not become bitter, and end up hating our white brothers."

To loud "amens" and shouts of encouragement from the audience, King ended his speech:

> If we protest courageously, and yet with dignity and Christian love, when the history books are written in the future, somebody will have to say, "There lived a race of people, of black people, of people who had the moral courage to stand up for their rights. And thereby they injected a new meaning into the veins of history and civilization.[34]

An emotionally wrought King sat down, too drained to fully bask in the raucous applause that bounded about the church and echoed outside. For the first time he had used the power of his brilliant oratory to move people. As he later recalled, no matter what the boycott's outcome, "the real victory was in the mass meeting, where thousands of black people stood revealed with a new sense of dignity and destiny."[35]

The MIA later announced its three main demands: Bus drivers must cease insulting black riders, passengers must be seated on a first-come, first-served basis (although as a conciliatory move they stated that blacks would start from the bus's back

and whites from the front), and the city had to hire black bus drivers for those routes most used by black riders.

The Boycott Stretches On

As expected, the bus company and city officials rejected MIA's three demands, so both sides settled into what was expected to be a lengthy boycott. The city first struck at black-owned taxi companies by reminding them that, by law, they had to charge a minimum fee. Any company officials who lowered prices would be subject to arrest.

To replace the taxi companies, blacks relied on an elaborate car pool system. Forty-eight dispatch and forty-two pickup stations offered riders a fairly comprehensive transportation system. Blacks of all backgrounds volunteered their time and their cars to drive other blacks to work.

Sometimes, though, it was the individual who resorted to walking who most moved King. One car pool driver spotted an elderly woman walking down the street and offered her a ride. She refused, saying, "I'm not walking for myself. I'm walking for my children and grandchildren." A few months after the boycott started King told a woman named Old Mother Pollard that "you have been with us all along, so now you go on and start ridin' the bus, 'cause you are too old to keep walking." Pollard answered that she would walk until the boycott ended. When an astonished King asked if her feet were tired, she replied, "Yes, my feet is tired, but my soul is rested." King, who claimed that the boycott was the story of black people who "were willing to substitute tired feet for tired souls," was uplifted by the heroic responses and started calling the bus boycott the "miracle of Montgomery."[36]

King held large meetings twice each week to keep participants informed. As the boycott dragged into weeks and then months without end in sight, he used these meetings to remind his followers that, though frustrated, they must adhere to Gandhi's nonviolent approach. To boost sagging morale, King exhorted, "We've got to keep on keepin' on, in order to gain freedom."[37]

His words touched listeners in unexpected ways. A journalist claimed King's voice could "charm your heart right out of your body." A woman who could not understand all of King's words gushed, "I don't know what that boy talkin' about, but I sure like the way he sounds." Another listener declared, "When I hears Dr. King, I see angel's wings flying 'round his head."[38]

Not every black approved of King. Some ministers thought that King loved the national attention the boycott brought him and that he eagerly sought headlines. Though hurt by this criticism, King tried to put it behind him.

When the boycott began, King expected that white ministers who preached kindness and fairness in their churches would support the action. Instead, he

Those who boycotted the buses set up car pool systems to help people get to work. If a car was not available, people walked.

received either outright hostility or apathy. Astonished that men of God would turn their backs on people in need, even people of a different color, King later claimed this assumption was his biggest mistake.

Threats and Bombings

Within one month of the boycott's start, King received as many as forty hate letters each day. Members of the Ku Klux Klan, devoted to suppressing any black pride, warned King to get out of town and threatened, "Did you know you only have a very short time to life [sic] if you dont quit your dam foolishness here in Montgomery?"[39]

Even worse were the twenty or more threatening phone calls, heavily peppered with hate and obscenity, he and his family were subjected to each day. Since he needed the telephone to coordinate the boycott, King could not remove the instrument, but he often wondered if he were doing the right thing by leading the Montgomery boycott because it endangered the lives of his family. The phone calls were so filled with venom that King and Coretta jumped whenever they heard the telephone ring.

One call in the middle of the night particularly rattled King. "Nigger, if you aren't out of this town in three days we gonna blow your brains out and blow up your house." King rose from bed, put on some coffee, and thought about what his leadership meant to his loved ones. He fell to his knees in despair and prayed:

Oh, Lord, I'm down here trying to do what is right. But, Lord, I must confess that I'm weak now. I'm afraid. The people are looking to me for leadership, and if I stand before them without strength and courage, they too will falter. I am at the end of my powers. I have nothing left. I can't face it alone.[40]

Suddenly, a calmness came over King, and he heard a voice tell him that he was not alone. He listened as words exhorted him to stand up for his beliefs and to trust that God would be at his side. King rose from his knees, reassured that all would be well.

Danger refused to leave so easily, however. Around 9:30 P.M. on January 30, 1956, with her husband away giving a speech, Coretta heard something hit the front porch of their home. As she hastened into a back room, an explosion tossed debris into the living room and filled the home with smoke.

As soon as King learned of the bomb, he left for home. Police officers had rushed to the scene to maintain calm, but by the time King arrived a sizable, angry crowd of supporters had gathered. One black man stared at a police officer and threatened, "You got your thirty-eight, and I got mine. Let's shoot it out."[41] Others walked around with clubs.

King emerged to tell his followers that his wife and child were unharmed. He reminded them that violence achieved nothing but more violence and asked them to disperse.

With his words, King defused a potential disaster. One policeman who stood outside that night later recalled, with an alarming mixture of gratefulness and bigotry, "I'll be honest with you. I was terrified. I owe my life to that nigger Preacher, and so do all the other white people who were there."[42]

On January 30, 1956, King's home was bombed. As an angry mob of his supporters formed outside the house, King urged them to remain calm.

Legal Maneuvers

Montgomery's white leadership attempted a variety of moves to end the boycott. In February 1956 the city government obtained indictments against King and eighty-eight other black leaders for breaking an obscure state law forbidding boycotts. King was in Atlanta when the charges were issued and planned to imme-

diately return, but his father, worried for his son's safety, argued against it. Daddy gathered some family friends, including the revered Dr. Mays from Morehouse College, in an effort to convince Martin that he should remain in Atlanta. "They gon' kill my boy,"[43] asserted Daddy to Atlanta's police chief, who agreed.

King listened to what the group said but claimed he could not shrink from his responsibility. "I must go back to Montgomery," he stated. "My friends and associates are being arrested. It would be the height of cowardice for me to stay away." Dr. Mays, who was moved by what his former pupil said, ended the discussion: "Martin must do what he feels is right. No great leader runs away from the battle."[44]

When King was found guilty in his March trial, his attorneys appealed the decision. City officials appealed another court ruling three months later when a group of federal judges declared Montgomery's segregated bus system unconstitutional. The case headed to the U.S. Supreme Court, where both sides knew the battle would be decided.

Meanwhile, city attorneys tried to get an injunction against the successful car pool system. If they could dismantle that device, they felt confident of outlasting the boycott, for Montgomery's blacks would have no alternative method of transportation. King worried that should the court agree with the city, many of his followers would start using the buses once again. They had valiantly battled for one year, and he knew he could not ask them to hold out for much longer.

In November 1956 the case went to court, but the drama ended faster than expected. While King waited for the decision, Rex Thomas, an Associated Press

After boycotting Alabama buses for a whole year, blacks finally won their case. In November 1956, the Supreme Court declared segregation on Alabama's buses unconstitutional. Signs like the one seen here were soon to become things of the past.

reporter, handed him a slip of paper. "Here is the decision that you have been waiting for. Read this release." King anxiously scanned the words to learn that the Supreme Court had declared unconstitutional Alabama's bus laws. "At this moment my heart began to throb with inexpressable joy,"[45] King later wrote. He had won.

Effects of the Boycott

While many southern whites reacted in disbelief and anger, King urged his followers to return to the buses with dignity. "I would be terribly disappointed if any of you go back to the buses bragging, 'We,

the Negroes, won a victory over the white people.' We must take this not as victory over the white man but as a victory for justice and democracy."[46]

In December King, Abernathy, and Parks boarded the bus in front of King's home. The bus driver smiled and said, "I believe you are Reverend King, aren't you?" When King answered he was, the driver added, "We are glad to have you this morning."[47] The trio sat in the bus's first row of seats, successfully ending with this simple action a year-long struggle for equality.

In recognition of his triumph, *Time* magazine placed King on its cover in February, concluding that "he struck where an attack was least expected, and where it hurt most: at the South's Christian conscience." The magazine quoted one white minister who said, "I know of very few white Southern ministers who aren't troubled and don't have admiration for King. They've become tortured souls."[48]

King's impact on black Americans extended beyond Montgomery's limits. For the first time the nation's blacks saw what could be accomplished with an organized force—without resorting to violence. Change could be made in decades-old institutions if one was willing to pay the price, and as a result, esteem for King soared in the nation. One black janitor boasted, "We got our heads up now, and we won't ever bow down again—no, sir— except before God!"[49] One member of King's Dexter congregation claimed that blacks had "never had anything to equal this in their whole lifetime. I don't believe that there is anything to equal the inspiration and hope and the love in this last one hundred years. He lifted them so high."[50]

One night, shortly after the boycott's end, forty carloads filled with Ku Klux Klan members drove through Montgomery's black neighborhoods in an attempt to emphasize that no matter what a court might decide, whites still held sway in Alabama. In prior years blacks would have remained in their homes until the Klan sped out of the area, but this night beaming black men, women, and children crowded onto front porches to wave to those who tried to intimidate them. A new day had dawned, filled with hope and pride.

4 "Injustice Anywhere Is a Threat"

Angry Southerners reacted violently to the desegregation of Montgomery's buses. In December gunfire showered city buses, and the next month unknown perpetrators firebombed four churches, including Ralph Abernathy's.

Appeal to the Government

King responded in typical fashion. He announced to his opponents that southern blacks would continue pressing for equal rights, even if it meant death or injury.

In early 1957 the African nation of Ghana, as part of its festivities celebrating its independence, invited King to speak. Since the country had struggled for equality in the past, King was delighted to accept. While in Ghana he met with U.S. vice president Richard M. Nixon and told him that he hoped one day to be celebrating in America the same kind of freedom that Ghana was then enjoying.

This statement was King's opening salvo in a campaign to enlist government support. Proclaiming that "injustice anywhere is a threat to justice everywhere,"[51] King hoped to prod a reluctant President Dwight D. Eisenhower into backing a strong civil rights bill. Though Eisen-

hower's version called for a commission to investigate attacks against civil rights, the president backed away from condemning school desegregation and unfair housing practices. After meeting the president, King claimed the leader was too conserva-

Martin Luther King Jr. believed that president Dwight D. Eisenhower (pictured) was too conservative in his approach to civil rights legislation.

tive to advocate true change. "Any evil facing the nation had to be extracted bit by bit with a tweezer because the surgeon's knife was an instrument too radical to touch this best of all possible societies,"[52] sighed King with obvious sarcasm. He knew that this attitude represented the beliefs of most of white America. He had many battles to fight before equality could be gained.

To promote a strong civil rights bill, King organized the Prayer Pilgrimage for Freedom. On May 17, 1957, twenty-five thousand people, including famous black personalities such as singer Harry Belafonte and baseball star Jackie Robinson, gathered at the steps of the Lincoln Memorial to hear King deliver his first national address. He delivered a stirring oration listing reasons why America needed to guarantee equal rights.

King moved people because he was able to crystallize complex issues in a few simple phrases. Where others fumbled to find the words to express their feelings, King smoothly glided through sentences and paragraphs. One man who worked with King, Rufus Lewis, contended that King's "greatest personal contribution was interpreting the situation to the mass of the people. He could speak better than any man that I've ever heard in expressing to the people their problem and making them see clearly what the situation was and inspiring them to work at it." A member of the Dexter congregation gushed to King one day, "Reverend, you have the words that we're thinking but can't say."[53]

While King was displeased that southern congressmen gutted many essential features from the final version of the 1957 Civil Rights Bill, he gave the law his lukewarm support. At least a commission fi-

nally existed that could investigate civil rights violations, and he decided that something was better than nothing.

The Southern Christian Leadership Conference

In August 1957 King took another step by forming the Southern Christian Leadership Conference (SCLC) to confront racial discrimination in the South. King established the SCLC because he believed the average black American needed another apparatus besides the NAACP, which worked mainly through the court system, and the Urban League, which focused on northern cities. Operating primarily through churches and espousing a nonviolent approach, the SCLC intended to bring activism to poor blacks as well as to wealthy ones, the family living in an Alabama shack or in a respectable neighborhood.

This move brought jealousy from other civil rights leaders, who hoped to organize their own methods of protest. A friend of King compared black leadership to a barrel of crabs: "King is the youngest crab and the others near the top are afraid he is going to pull them down on his way up."[54] For much of his career, King had to contend with criticism from other civil rights personalities.

The more famous King became, the more exposed he was to threats and attacks. In September 1958 he traveled to Montgomery to support Ralph Abernathy in a court case. As King walked toward the courthouse a guard warned him to turn back or he would be apprehended. Within seconds, and while a news photographer captured the infamous moment on film, a

While visiting Montgomery in September 1958 to support Ralph Abernathy in a legal case, King was arrested after refusing to obey the orders of a courthouse guard.

police officer grabbed King, harshly twisted his arm behind his back, and arrested him.

When a higher-ranking officer recognized King at the police station, he was quickly released, but the harm had been done. The photograph appeared the next day in hundreds of newspaper front pages across the nation, earning much sympathy for King and his cause. A judge later found King guilty of loitering and ordered him to pay a fourteen-dollar fine,

but King declared that he would accept jail before the fine. To avoid further national embarrassment, a Montgomery city official paid the fine.

Later that same month, King sat in a New York department store autographing copies of his first book, *Stride Toward Freedom,* which had been published earlier that spring. Izola Curry, a middle-aged black woman with mental problems, approached the table, yanked out a seven-inch-long letter opener, and stabbed King in the chest.

An ambulance sped King, with the letter opener still protruding from his chest, to Harlem Hospital. A team of surgeons, led by Dr. Aubré D. Maynard, removed one of King's ribs and part of his breastbone to retract the weapon, which had barely missed severing an aorta. Had that occurred, King would have bled to death before reaching the hospital.

Dr. Maynard spoke with the recovering King and informed him how close he had come to dying. Maynard explained that, with the letter opener's tip so close to his aorta, "If you had sneezed during all those hours of waiting, your aorta would have been punctured and you would have drowned in your own blood."[55]

News of King's wound brought a torrent of get-well wishes from across the nation. One letter especially moved King:

I am a ninth grade student at the White Plains High School. While it shouldn't matter, I would like to mention that I'm a white girl. I read in the paper of your misfortune and of your suffering. And I read that if you had sneezed you would have died. I'm simply writing to say that I'm so happy that you didn't sneeze.[56]

King's Philosophy

In February 1959 King visited India, where Mahatma Gandhi had achieved so much through nonviolence. He returned with a renewed determination to succeed in similar fashion in the United States, and he told trusted aides:

> We have a power, power that can't be found in Molotov cocktails, but we do have a power. Power that cannot be found in bullets and guns, but we have a power. It is a power as old as the insights of Jesus of Nazareth and as modern as the techniques of Mahatma Gandhi.[57]

King asserted that nonviolence, rather than a cowardly submission to evil, was the most courageous form of opposition one could employ. It asked the individual to risk injury or death without striking back. He urged his people to maintain the attitude that "I will not fight but I will not comply" with injustice. He added that some will pay the ultimate sacrifice, but "if such physical death is the price that we must pay to free our children from a life of permanent psychological death, then nothing could be more honorable."[58]

King claimed that every preacher had a moral obligation to work for change: "We cannot preach the gospel in the four walls of the church and let it stop there."[59]

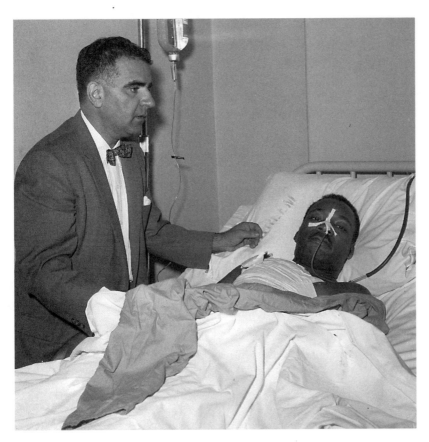

On September 20, 1958, a mentally disturbed woman made an attempt on King's life with a letter opener. The weapon came so close to his aorta that, as his doctor later told him, King (pictured here in Harlem Hospital) would have died if he had so much as sneezed while waiting for surgery.

Too often, King stated, ministers preached justice on Sundays and ignored it the rest of the week. Rather than lead, churches have "too often been a taillight rather than a headlight, and it's time for the church to be a headlight on all these problems that we face."[60]

A dire need was to register blacks to vote. Denied that basic right for decades through unfair practices in the South, blacks had never utilized the strength that a group could wield when it voted as a unit. King wanted to double the number of black voters before the 1960 presidential election so that politicians would take notice and begin to listen to black America.

With his responsibilities growing weekly, and because headquarters for the SCLC were in Atlanta, King decided that he had to move back to his hometown. After making the arrangements, including being named copastor at Ebenezer by an elated Daddy King, in late January 1960 King delivered his final sermon at Dexter. As he explained to an emotional congregation, "I can't stop now. History has thrust something upon me which I cannot turn away."[61]

The Sit-Ins Begin

The next month a new phenomenon captured the nation's interest when four black college students, enraged that lunch counters throughout the South denied service

Martin Luther King Jr. and his wife Coretta are greeted in India during their visit in February 1959. King's inspiration and determination were refreshed by his journey to the homeland of his role model, Mahatma Gandhi.

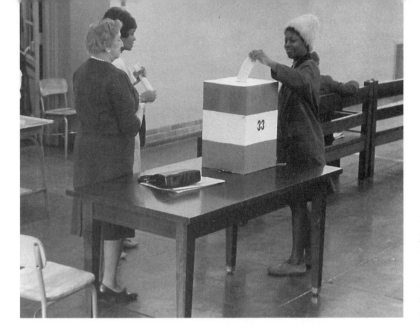

King wanted to tap into the political power that the black community could wield by voting. Throughout his campaigns for civil rights, he encouraged black people to register to vote.

to black customers, refused to leave Woolworth's lunch counter in Greensboro, North Carolina. The four courageously remained in their seats, despite being threatened and spat upon by hostile whites. Word quickly spread to other portions of the South, causing other college students to do the same in their towns. Since the sit-ins cut into the businesses' profits, within a relatively short time 126 southern towns desegregated their lunch counters.

Though he had not organized the sit-ins, King admired the students' bravery and fully supported their efforts. He met

---

Sit-Ins

King hoped to find other nonviolent means of opposing segregation besides marches. Taylor Branch records the account of the first sit-in in his book Parting the Waters: America in the King Years, 1954–1963.

"That same night of Monday, February 1, students at the Negro colleges around Greensboro, North Carolina, were electrified by reports of what four freshman boys had done that day. . . . The four of them had gone to the downtown Woolworth's store and slipped into the seats at the sacrosanct whites-only lunch counter. The Negro waitress had said, 'Fellows like you make our race look bad,' and refused to serve them, but the four freshmen had not only sat there unperturbed all afternoon but also promised to return at ten o'clock the next morning to continue what they called a 'sit-down protest.'"

with student leaders in April and offered them whatever assistance they required. Rather than become a portion of the SCLC, the students organized the Student Nonviolent Coordinating Committee (SNCC) and appointed King to its advisory board.

The students practically forced King's hand on his next move when they targeted Atlanta for sit-ins in October. Along with Atlanta's other black ministers, King had agreed with city leaders to ignore the town's segregated policies as long as gradual progress was made in that area. Suddenly, exuberant college students poured into town with the expectation that King would solidly support them.

Seeing no alternative, King joined the students on October 19, 1960, at the area's largest department store, Rich's. Though blacks could purchase items at the store, they could not sit at the lunch counter or even try on clothes before purchasing them. Rich's owners believed white customers would refuse to buy clothes that had been worn by black buyers.

King was arrested along with the other protesters and thrown into jail. While Atlanta officials hoped to quickly release King, authorities in neighboring De Kalb County wanted him handed over. King had earlier been pulled over for speeding in the county; as part of his sentence, he was placed on a one-year probation. Since he had now been arrested a second time, De Kalb officials claimed King had violated the terms of his probation.

King and his lawyers feared the move, for De Kalb was an infamous Klan stronghold. On the night of October 25, deputies picked up King and drove him to Reidsville Penitentiary, a cockroach-ridden cesspool known for its brutality to black prisoners.

At one point King believed that he was going to die, but a rising politician came to

King Goes to Jail

In his account of the civil rights movement, They Had a Dream: The Civil Rights Struggle, *Jules Archer tells of an incident involving King's daughter.*

"After a week in jail [for his part in a sit-in] Martin was released. But just as soon as he emerged, he was rearrested by the sheriff of De Kalb County, a Ku Klux Klan stronghold, on a trumped-up charge. Sentenced to six months of hard labor in the state penitentiary at Reidsville, Georgia, he was taken there in handcuffs and leg chains.

When wire services reported the arrest of the famous black civil rights leader, a little white girl sneered to Martin's five-year-old daughter Yoki [Yolanda], 'Oh, your daddy is *always* going to jail!'

'Yes,' Yoki replied proudly, 'he goes to jail to help people.'"

John F. Kennedy (at podium), with the help of his brother Robert (seated, second from left), acted to get King released from Reidsville Penitentiary. Kennedy later was elected president, and King finally felt he had an ally in the White House.

his assistance. Massachusetts senator John F. Kennedy, the Democratic Party's nominee for the 1960 presidential election, called Coretta King to inquire about her husband. When Kennedy learned where King had been taken, he ordered his brother and campaign manager, Robert, to call the De Kalb County judge who had placed King behind bars and convey his displeasure.

The pressure applied by Kennedy worked wonders, and King was released within twenty-four hours. King returned to Atlanta, where he told a throng of supporters, "It took a lot of courage for Senator Kennedy to do this, especially in Georgia."[62] Kennedy's quick action, with the election only a few days away, gained him enormous popularity among black citizens and helped swing the election to the Democrats. King now believed civil rights had a friend in the White House.

Eventually Atlanta city officials agreed to a plan that would desegregate downtown lunch counters by September 1961. With success achieved in his hometown, King now turned his attention to bus facilities throughout the South.

Freedom Riders

In the spring of 1961 King met the newly elected president, John Kennedy, at the White House. While King hoped that Kennedy would aggressively pursue civil rights, the president explained that he had to wait until he had more support in Congress. As it stood, southern senators and representatives would thwart his every move should he try to push through far-reaching legislation. Kennedy did promise to appoint blacks to high administrative

In an effort to see if the South would comply with legislation banning segregation on transportation that crossed state lines, a group called the Freedom Riders traveled in two buses from Washington, D.C., to Alabama. In Anniston, Alabama, one of the vehicles was attacked by racists and burned.

posts and to open talks with southern officials about quickening the pace of desegregating their facilities.

In December 1960 the U.S. Supreme Court outlawed segregation in railroad stations, bus terminals, and trains and buses that crossed state lines. A group organized by the Congress of Racial Equality (CORE) planned to test whether the South intended to obey the ruling by sending two busloads of riders into different southern towns. Dubbed Freedom Riders, the group drove from Washington, D.C., to Anniston, Alabama, where a hostile white mob burned one of the buses.

The second bus continued to Birmingham, Alabama. Local KKK members, wielding baseball bats, iron pipes, and chains, eagerly waited for the bus, as the police agreed to stay away from the area for fifteen minutes to give the organization time to "greet" the arrivals. When the bus pulled into the station, the KKK bashed, kicked, and punched their way through the Freedom Riders in a horrendous display of violence.

Robert Kennedy, now the nation's top law enforcement official as the attorney general, arranged for a new bus to transport the Freedom Riders to Montgomery,

Alabama. The result was the same, as an emotional crowd of one thousand whites immediately attacked the hapless riders, shouting, "Get them niggers!" and "Kill the nigger-loving son-of-a-bitch!"[63] An appalled Robert Kennedy immediately dispatched five hundred federal marshals to the Montgomery area to restore order.

King, sheltered by fifty U.S. marshals, flew into Montgomery to speak at Ralph Abernathy's church. As he spoke on May 20, a hostile crowd formed outside and began hurling racial slurs and rocks through the church windows. Some threatened to burn the church. The mob's angry mood deepened each minute, and even though federal marshals ringed the church, King and the others inside feared for their safety. Could they count on white marshals to shield them from a huge white mob?

From inside the church, King telephoned the attorney general to express his apprehension over their safety. Robert Kennedy assured him the marshals would protect the group, and though the violent night terrified the church's occupants, by 5:00 A.M. marshals had dispersed the crowds and were able to safely escort everyone out of the area.

The Freedom Riders planned to head on to Mississippi, but King declined to travel with them. Events throughout the South were rapidly escalating, but if he accompanied the Freedom Riders he might

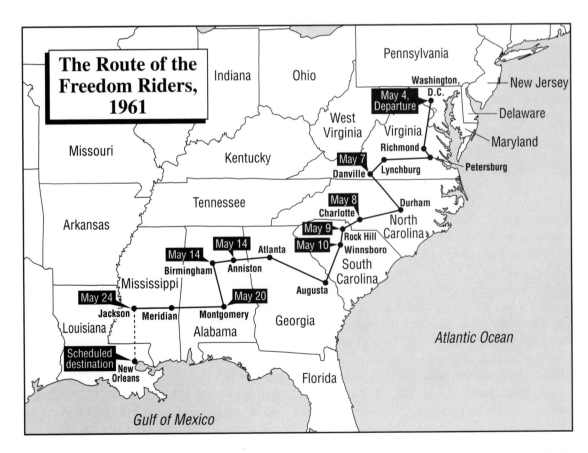

The Route of the Freedom Riders, 1961

be imprisoned for violating his parole. Though he tried to explain his predicament to the young civil rights workers, he failed to sway them. One said with disgust, "I would rather have heard King say, 'I'm scared—that's why I'm not going.'"[64]

Despite the unfortunate ending, the Freedom Riders succeeded in bringing change when Robert Kennedy ordered the Interstate Commerce Commission to issue regulations ending segregation in bus terminals. Gradually, those hateful Whites Only signs disappeared.

The Freedom Riders triumphed, in part, because they had been followed by the national press. Reporters wrote stories about the hostile receptions and photographers and television cameras captured images of hate on film. People across the country read and watched with revulsion, thereby swinging more support to civil rights advocates. Impressed by this, King planned to make more efficient use of the media in future campaigns.

Failure at Albany and a Loss of Face

In the summer of 1961 SNCC organized a voter registration drive in Albany, Georgia. By year's end almost 500 blacks sat in Georgia jails for their roles in this campaign, so King and Abernathy traveled to Albany to lead a march on city hall. As the 250 people walked toward their destination, Albany police, led by chief of police Laurie Pritchett, stopped them. Rather than employ violence as had occurred in most other locations, Pritchett gave his men strict orders to treat the marchers with respect. He intended to avoid the

negative publicity that violent outbursts garnered in the national media. When King and the others refused to disband, Pritchett's men politely herded them into police vehicles and drove them to jail.

After spending two days in jail, King was told that a settlement had been reached between city officials and local blacks, so he posted bond and left Albany. Unfortunately, King had been tricked—no agreement had been signed at all. He tried to regain momentum by returning to Albany, but he failed. Many in SNCC thought King had deserted them when they most needed him.

Albany was not King's finest hour. The New York *Herald-Tribune* wrote that Albany was "a devastating loss of face" for King that represented "one of the most stunning defeats"[65] of his career. Even worse, Police Chief Pritchett gloated that Albany remained as segregated as ever.

Family Matters Suffer

The second problem King faced was finding time to spend with his family. The pressures of coordinating civil rights activities in different locations, of answering letters and phone calls, of preparing and delivering speeches, consumed vast chunks of time, and King struggled to save some for Coretta and the children. Unfortunately, it rarely was enough.

Sometimes his moments with the children could be agonizing. Each time they drove to Atlanta's airport they passed by a segregated amusement park called Funtown. As King told an interviewer, "Yolanda would inevitably say, 'I want to go to Funtown,' and I would always evade a direct reply. I really didn't know how to ex-

What Do You Say?

King explained in a 1965 Playboy *magazine interview how inarticulate he became when his own children asked him why they could not enter certain southern businesses. This excerpt is taken from editor James Melvin Washington's book* A Testament of Hope: The Essential Writings and Speeches of Martin Luther King Jr.

"I have won some applause as a speaker, but my tongue twisted and my speech stammered seeking to explain to my six-year-old daughter why the public invitation on television [to come to Funtown] didn't include her, and others like her. One of the most painful experiences I have ever faced was to see her tears when I told her that Funtown was closed to colored children, for I realized that at that moment the first dark cloud of inferiority had floated into her little mental sky, that at that moment her personality had begun to warp with that first unconscious bitterness toward white people. It was the first time that prejudice based upon skin color had been explained to her."

King (seen here with his daughter at the 1964 World's Fair in New York) had a difficult time explaining to his children why they could not visit similar places in the South.

plain to her why she couldn't go." Though he eventually found the words to tell his daughter, he did not want her to become bitter, so he added that while "many white people were against her going to Funtown, there were many others who *did* want colored children to go."[66]

Later, when King was jailed in Albany, Yolanda cried for her father and said she missed him. Coretta explained that her father was in jail so that everyone, no matter the color, could go wherever they wanted. Yolanda shot back, "Good, tell him to stay in jail until I can go to Funtown."[67]

5 "'Wait' Has Almost Always Meant 'Never'"

In September 1962 King spoke in Birmingham, Alabama, at the SCLC's annual convention. The organization selected Birmingham because the city's blacks had instituted a boycott against white merchants, and the SCLC hoped to draw attention to the situation.

As King talked, a white youth leaped onstage and attacked him. The youth was quickly subdued, but King told the police to let him go. As King explained, "This system that we live under creates people such as this youth. I'm not interested in pressing charges. I'm interested in changing the kind of system that produces this kind of man." [68]

Though he did not know it at the time, King would soon return to Birmingham and produce one of the civil rights movement's most dramatic episodes.

The Birmingham Campaign

As 1963 approached, momentum for change gained such speed that the year became one of the most memorable in American history. At first ecstatic with the 1954 Supreme Court decision that banned school segregation, blacks had since been disillusioned with the slow pace of imple-

mentation. In the nine years since, only 9 percent of southern blacks attended integrated schools.

At the same time, blacks elsewhere in the world achieved significant gains as European nations that once controlled Africa yielded power to newly formed countries. King wrote that "the Negro saw black statesmen voting on vital issues in the United Nations—and knew that in many cities of his own land he was not permitted to take that significant walk to the ballot box." [69]

These factors assumed even greater significance in 1963, exactly one hundred years after Abraham Lincoln signed the historic Emancipation Proclamation to end slavery during the Civil War. Most blacks believed the time had come to produce significant, lasting changes.

King felt an even more personal reason: In March 1963 he and Coretta celebrated the birth of their fourth child—daughter Bernice Albertine. Later that year, however, the Lovett School in Atlanta, an Episcopalian school, refused to accept son Marty because of his color. King could only wonder when his little boy could attend any school or when his small daughter could freely walk into any amusement park in the land.

For his next action, King and his advisers chose Birmingham. Calling the town "the most thoroughly segregated city in the country,"[70] King knew that if the SCLC could make progress there, it could make it anywhere. Blacks lived in fear of the white establishment, led by the bigoted commissioner of public safety T. Eugene "Bull" Connor, who gave his police force a free hand to use violence and intimidation to keep "niggers" in their place. He announced that he would not allow any of the civil rights nonsense occurring elsewhere to invade Birmingham, and he swore that "blood would run in the streets"[71] should King or others try anything.

With such an obstinate foe boldly issuing threats, King realized that the national press would descend on Birmingham to cover a civil rights march. Their cameras and pens would record every instance and broadcast it to the country and world. He hoped that this widespread attention would create new momentum to eliminate segregation in the South. As he said, "TV is going to be the medium in which we bring this country face-to-face with itself."[72]

King Is Arrested

King opened the campaign on April 3 by announcing three demands in the "Birmingham Manifesto": All downtown lunch counters, rest rooms, and drinking fountains must be desegregated; local businesses must hire blacks; and a biracial committee to discuss civil rights matters must be formed. Until these demands were met, blacks would boycott city businesses and conduct marches.

Two days later King warned the marchers to maintain calm but to be prepared to acccept a heavy price for their actions:

And I know when I say don't be afraid, you know what I mean. Don't even be

T. Eugene "Bull" Connor leads Birmingham, Alabama, police in a mass arrest of people protesting segregation in May 1963. Connor vowed he would not let any civil rights "nonsense" invade Birmingham.

afraid to die. I submit to you tonight that no man is free if he fears death. But the minute you conquer the fear of death, at that moment you are free. You must say somehow, I don't have much money; I don't have much education; I may not be able to read and write; but I have the capacity to die.[73]

King faced a dilemma in the first week. Each day the black men and women who marched or selected a business for a sit-in were arrested by an unusually peaceful Bull Connor and his police, then bailed out of jail by SCLC funds. To raise additional money to fuel the drive, King planned to conduct a national speaking tour. However, a judge granted a city injunction prohibiting King, Abernathy, and other leaders from conducting further marches or sit-ins. If King disobeyed the order, he would be imprisoned and unable to raise much-needed funds.

He agonized over this issue. Where would his movement receive money if he were locked up? After praying for guidance, King decided that he had to trust that things would work out, donned a pair of coveralls, and prepared to march.

On April 12, Good Friday, King and Abernathy led fifty people on a march to city hall, where police promptly arrested them. For twenty-four hours Coretta King had no contact with her husband, who received verbal abuse and harsh treatment from his jailers. Worried for her husband's safety, Coretta contacted the White House on Easter Sunday. The president was not in, but within a few hours his brother, Robert, returned her call with the information that King was safe and would be calling her soon.

Suddenly, the jailers reacted with more courtesy and allowed King to phone his wife. When he learned what Robert Kennedy had done on his behalf, he ordered his aides to spread that information to every news reporter so that everyone would know that the federal government was keeping a close eye on Birmingham.

"Letter from Birmingham Jail"

Though King remained in jail, he was in close touch with events occurring outside. In fact, one of his most eloquent statements on behalf of civil rights took place in his jail cell. On April 13 the Birmingham *News* printed a story titled, "White Clergymen Urge Local Negroes to Withdraw from Demonstrations." Signed by eight liberal clergymen who had earlier risked their reputations and lives by opposing Alabama governor George Wallace's obstinate stand favoring segregation, the article condemned King's actions because of the vehement backlash they produced from local whites. The clergymen concluded that "such actions as incite hatred and violence, however technically peaceful those actions may be, have not contributed to the resolution of our local problems."[74]

Appalled, but not surprised that Christian ministers would attack his nonviolent movement, King crafted a response. Writing on anything that his aides could smuggle into his jail cell, including toilet paper, scraps of paper, and on any free space on newspaper pages, King penned page after page. Swept along by the urgency of responding to fellow ministers, King seemed lifted to new heights in his ability to eloquently summarize why he and others battled for civil rights.

Martin Luther King and Ralph Abernathy are taken into custody after leading a demonstration in Birmingham on Good Friday, 1963. They wore old clothes to dramatize the boycott against racist business practices.

King Answers from Jail

King created one of the most eloquent statements on behalf of civil rights when he wrote to the white Birmingham ministers from his jail cell. He hoped the ministers would receive his letter in the spirit of openness and cooperation, but King never received a reply. In his ending to the letter, found in his book "Letter from Birmingham Jail" and "I Have a Dream" Speech, King extended the hand of friendship.

"If I have said anything in this letter that overstates the truth and indicates an unreasonable impatience, I beg you to forgive me. If I have said anything that understates the truth and indicates my having a patience that allows me to settle for anything less than brotherhood, I beg God to forgive me. . . .

Let us all hope that the dark clouds of racial prejudice will soon pass away and the deep fog of misunderstanding will be lifted from our fear-drenched communities, and in some not too distant tomorrow the radiant stars of love and brotherhood will shine over our great nation with all their scintillating beauty."

Martin Luther King alone with his thoughts in a Birmingham jail cell, November 1967.

To the charge that King brought only trouble to Birmingham, a city that was not even his home, King answered that he was there because injustice was there. "I cannot sit idly by in Atlanta and not be concerned about what happens in Birmingham," King wrote. He then added one of his favorite statements, "Injustice anywhere is a threat to justice everywhere."

"An Unjust Law Is No Law at All"

The clergy wondered why King was not willing to wait until various Birmingham political and civic groups decided how best to implement desegregation. King had heard that refrain all his life—if only blacks would wait a while longer, conditions would improve. He produced a devastating response:

> We know through painful experience that freedom is never voluntarily given by the oppressor; it must be demanded by the oppressed. . . . For years now I have heard the word "Wait!" It rings in the ear of every Negro with piercing familiarity. This "Wait" has almost always meant "Never." We must come to see . . . that "justice too long delayed is justice denied."

King pointed to gains toward independence made "with jetlike speed" by African people, "but we still creep at horse-and-buggy pace toward gaining a cup of coffee at a lunch counter."

In some of his most famous words, King tried to convey to the white clergy why a sense of urgency propelled black Americans:

Perhaps it is easy for those who have never felt the stinging darts of segregation to say, "Wait." But when you have seen vicious mobs lynch your mothers and fathers at will and drown your sisters and brothers at whim; when you have seen hate-filled policemen curse, kick, and even kill your black brothers and sisters; when you see the vast majority of your twenty million Negro brothers smothering in an airtight cage of poverty in the midst of an affluent society; . . . when you are humiliated day in and day out by nagging signs reading "white" and "colored"; when your first name becomes "nigger," your middle name becomes "boy" (however old you are) and your last name becomes "John,". . . when you are forever fighting a degenerating sense of "nobodiness"—then you will understand why we find it difficult to wait. There comes a time when the cup of endurance runs over, and men are no longer willing to be plunged into the abyss of despair.

The clergymen asked King how he could obey some laws yet break others and still remain a just man. From his cell King answered that "there are two types of laws: just and unjust. . . . One has not only a legal but a moral responsibility to obey just laws. Conversely, one has a moral responsibility to disobey unjust laws." He turned to a famous theologian for support by quoting St. Augustine's conclusion that "an unjust law is no law at all."

King shattered the contention that his actions created violence: "Isn't this like condemning a robbed man because his possession of money precipitated the evil act of robbery?"

Demonstrators in Birmingham take refuge in a doorway as firemen blast them with water from high-pressure hoses. Intended to break up the protest, actions such as this only strengthened support for the civil rights movement.

King ended his lengthy letter by stating,

Let us all hope that the dark clouds of racial prejudice will soon pass away and the deep fog of misunderstanding will be lifted from our fear-drenched communities, and in some not too distant tomorrow the radiant stars of love and brotherhood will shine over our great nation with all their scintillating beauty.[75]

King never received a reply to his passionate appeal for equality, but the civil rights movement now owned a powerful statement of beliefs. King had clearly expressed what so many other people felt but could not put into words.

Enter the Children

On April 20 King and Abernathy posted bond and walked out of jail. Unfortunately, rather than march and risk arrest, many blacks had remained quietly out of sight and thus endangered the campaign's success. King had to quickly think of some remedy to avoid a complete collapse that, occurring so soon after the Albany disaster, could seriously impede his ability to lead. Since a sufficient number of adults would not place their bodies on the line, King turned to the only other group of blacks available—Birmingham's grade school and high school students.

They responded in droves as more than one thousand black youths between the ages of six and sixteen gathered for the May 2 march. Watching with his police force, an exasperated Connor vowed that the "little niggers," as he labeled them, would be quickly arrested. Though he carried out that threat and sent many to jail, the next day an even larger group of young children and teenagers collected for a second march. Flushed with anger, Connor ordered his men to use force to break up the march.

What followed stunned the nation. Police officers, clutching leashes holding snarling German shepherd attack dogs, and firemen manning powerful fire hoses, waited for the order. As the marchers drew closer, some teens shouted insults and others hurled rocks or bottles toward their adversaries. Connor, growing angrier by the second, sent in his men and the dogs.

Within moments chaos reigned as police dogs chased frightened boys and girls and stinging streams of water from fire hoses battered others to the ground. To increase the potency of his hoses, Connor employed a specially designed monitor gun that combined the thrust from two fire hoses into one nozzle with such force that it could strip bark from trees one hundred feet away. A leading black businessman, A. G. Gaston, watched from his offices above the fray while firemen sprayed the marchers. "They've turned the fire hoses on a little black girl," he cried to a friend. "And they're rolling that girl right down the middle of the street."[76] The crowd scattered in all directions in a futile attempt to avoid the biting dogs and club-swinging policemen.

Some public figures criticized King for using the children. Robert Kennedy

The Children Join In

One of the most moving portions of the Birmingham campaign was when the city's youthful blacks poured onto the streets to support the adults. Taylor Branch describes the event in his book Parting the Waters: America in the King Years, 1954–1963.

"Except for the absence of adults in the line, it seemed to be another day in the month-long siege until a second double line of marchers spilled out through the church's front doors. Shortly after them came another group, followed by another and another. . . . Police radios crackled with requests for more paddy wagons. . . .

From the swirling mass of Negro children, blue uniforms, and picket signs, an anxious policeman spotted a familiar figure across the Sixteenth Street truce line. 'Hey, Fred,' he called. 'How many more have you got?'

'At least a thousand!' shouted Shuttlesworth [a civil rights leader].

'God Almighty,' said the policeman."

claimed that "school children participating in street demonstrations is a dangerous business. An injured, maimed or dead child is a price that none of us can afford to pay."[77] Though stung by these and other harsh words, King wondered where their concern was when the same black children had been forced to use inferior rest rooms and substandard schools through the years.

Though he did not realize it, Connor brought more sympathy and support to the civil rights movement. Horrified reporters and photographers recorded the incident, and when television audiences across the country watched the coverage, they pulled back in revulsion. People may view one adult harming another without becoming overly emotional, but the image of Birmingham's adults attacking Birmingham's children was more than most could accept. Each time the image of a bleeding child flashed across television screens, the civil rights movement gained momentum. Each time that fire hoses stung their faces and backs, bigotry lost an advocate. As King recalled, "When a police dog buried his fangs in the ankle of a small child in Birmingham, he buried his fangs in the ankle of every American."[78] An enraged President Kennedy dispatched the assistant attorney general, Burke Marshall, to Birmingham with orders to negotiate a speedy settlement.

Connor failed to stop the children. Each day produced a new group of marchers who braved the dogs and fire hoses, and each day photographers recorded it for the world. Certain moments moved King to tears, such as the girl, no more than eight years old, who was

Two youths find temporary shelter from the fire hoses behind a large tree. King was later criticized by some for putting children at risk during the demonstration in Birmingham.

President John F. Kennedy speaks to the country on national television on June 11, 1963. He stated that the time for sweeping civil rights legislation was at hand.

men. The two groups stared at each other for a time, then the boys and girls continued walking toward the police, "and Connor's men fell back as though hypnotized, as the Negroes marched on past to hold their prayer meeting. I saw there, I felt there, for the first time, the pride and the power,"[81] related King.

Victory in Birmingham

Hurt by financial losses to the business community and eager to deflect the worldwide criticism, Birmingham's white business leaders opened negotiations. On May 10 they agreed to King's demands for desegregation in public areas and for the hiring of blacks.

The impact traveled to Washington, D.C., where President Kennedy believed the time had come to ask Congress for a strong civil rights bill outlawing segregation in interstate public accommodations, handing power to the attorney general to bring suits against districts with segregated schools, and stopping the flow of federal money to any project that refused to hire minorities. Kennedy spelled out his proposals in a nationally televised address on June 11, 1963, in which he reminded Americans that the time had arrived for equal rights and asked, "Who among us would be content to have the color of his skin changed and stand in his place? Who among us would then be content with the counsels of patience and delay?"[82]

As so frequently occurred in King's life, his moments of triumph seemed stalked by tragedy that followed in their aftermaths. One day after the successful Birmingham agreement, opponents tossed

mockingly asked by a club-wielding police officer why she bothered to march. The little girl gazed into the officer's eyes and replied with the simple word, "F'eedom." King later wrote that "she could not even pronounce the word, but no Gabriel trumpet could have sounded a truer note."[79] Throughout his career, King recalled this instance when events appeared bleak. "Many times when I have been in sorely trying situations, the memory of that little one has come into my mind, and has buoyed me."[80]

Another incident illustrated the power of nonviolence. Three thousand youths marched toward a prayer meeting when they encountered Bull Connor and his

NAACP leader Medgar Evers was gunned down by a racist in Mississippi in 1963. Unfortunately, he would not be the last casualty in the fight for equality.

organizer Medgar Evers as he walked toward his front door. Gains would be made, but a terrible price had to be paid.

King was again surprised by the apathy of many whites. Though they apparently knew segregation was wrong, white moderates refused to speak out; thus, Connor and his type remained in power until King's marches brought change. As King later said, "The ultimate tragedy of Birmingham was not the brutality of the bad people, but the silence of the good people."[83] For his entire career, King never could understand why so many decent people allowed evil to run rampant without uttering a sound.

Despite these troubling points, Birmingham was a resounding triumph; it not only changed city practices, it also proved that a united black community could successfully assert its desires, even in such a southern bastion as Birmingham. Connor's brutal tactics helped pave the way—President Kennedy later mentioned to King, partly in jest, that "the civil rights movement owes Bull Connor as much as it owes Abraham Lincoln"[84]—but victory came because people who had endured decades of abuse said no more.

Much work remained, however. After Birmingham, King quoted what a slave had said right after the Civil War: "We ain't what we ought to be and we ain't what we want to be and we ain't what we're going to be. But thank God we ain't what we was."[85]

bombs through A. D. King's house and into the Gaston Motel, where King had stayed. Though King had returned to Atlanta, he quickly flew into Birmingham to stem the violence that had erupted. Shortly after Kennedy's civil rights speech, a Mississippi bigot gunned down NAACP

6 "Let Freedom Ring"

Heartened by Birmingham, blacks across the South staged sit-ins and other protests throughout the summer of 1963. As a result, over 250 cities desegregated their public facilities. However, greater strides needed to be achieved since numerous southern cities still closed parks, hotels, and other locations to blacks.

"I Have a Dream"

To dramatically expose segregation, King and other leaders planned a gigantic summer march on Washington, D.C. On August 28, 1963, 250,000 people, including celebrities such as Harry Belafonte, actors Paul Newman and Burt Lancaster, and baseball great Jackie Robinson, gathered along the reflecting pool stretching from the Washington Monument to the Lincoln Memorial to listen to various civil rights leaders speak.

Unable to attend, James Farmer of CORE sent a message stating that "We will not stop until the dogs stop biting us in the South and the rats stop biting us in the North [in slums]."[86] Other individuals either spoke or sang to the throng as morning wound into afternoon on the steamy summer day. Finally King, with the famous statue of Lincoln hovering behind him, stepped to the podium.

Some, impatient with the program's slow pace, had started to drift away as King uttered his first words. "Five score years ago, a great American, in whose symbolic shadow we stand today, signed the Emancipation Proclamation. This momentous decree came as a great beacon light of hope to millions of Negro slaves who had been seared in the flames of withering injustice."

People stopped moving, drawn by the power of King's voice and the poetry of his words: "But one hundred years later, the Negro is still not free. One hundred years later, the life of the Negro is still sadly crippled by the manacles of segregation and the chains of discrimination."

Movement in the crowd slowed, then ceased as King's rich voice fluttered across the mall, and within moments King's inspiring oratory carried each man, woman, and child on an emotional ride. He answered those who wondered when blacks would be satisfied by stating, "We can never be satisfied as long as our children are stripped of their selfhood and robbed of their dignity by signs stating 'for whites only.'"

He then launched into the most eloquent portion of his most famous speech. To resounding "Amens!" and cries of support, King offered hope to the throng:

A crowd of 250,000 people gather around the reflecting pool in Washington, D.C., on August 28, 1963. It was here, in the shadow of the Lincoln Memorial, that King gave his famous "I Have a Dream" speech.

So I say to you, my friends, that even though we must face the difficulties of today and tomorrow, I still have a dream. It is a dream deeply rooted in the American dream that one day this nation will rise up and live out the true meaning of its creed—we hold these truths to be self-evident, that all men are created equal.

To the crowd's murmurs of approval, King continued:

I have a dream that one day on the red hills of Georgia, sons of former slaves and sons of former slave-owners will be able to sit down together at the table of brotherhood.

I have a dream that one day, even the state of Mississippi, a state sweltering with the heat of injustice, sweltering with the heat of oppression, will be transformed into an oasis of freedom and justice.

I have a dream my four little children will one day live in a nation where they will not be judged by the color of their skin but by the content of their character. I have a dream today!

I have a dream that one day, down in Alabama, with its vicious racists, . . . little black boys and black girls will be able to join hands with little white boys and white girls as sisters and brothers. I have a dream today!

The crowd hung on each word and every phrase as King swept them along with his thundering proclamations. He then came to the end:

Let freedom ring from the mighty mountains of New York. Let freedom ring from the heightening Alleghenies of Pennsylvania. Let freedom ring from the snow-capped Rockies of Colorado. Let freedom ring from the curvaceous slopes of California. But not only that. Let freedom ring from Stone Mountain of Georgia. Let freedom ring from Lookout Mountain of Tennessee. Let freedom ring from every hill and molehill of Mississippi, from every mountainside, let freedom ring.

And when this happens, and when we allow freedom to ring, when we let it ring from every village and hamlet,

Martin Luther King Jr. delivers his address at the Lincoln Memorial. King called this march the "greatest demonstration of freedom in the history of our nation."

from every state and city, we will be able to speed up that day when all of God's children—black men and white men, Jews and Gentiles, Catholics and Protestants—will be able to join hands and to sing in the words of the old Negro spiritual, "Free at last, free at last; thank God Almighty, we are free at last."[87]

A quarter of a million people cheered and applauded in unison as King finished his famous speech. Men and women, young and old, felt they had a say in their futures—one day conditions would be better for themselves and their children. As writer James Baldwin claims, "That day, for a moment, it almost seemed that we stood on a height, and could see our inheritance. Perhaps we could make the Kingdom real, perhaps the beloved community would not forever remain the dream one dreamed in agony."[88]

The Death of Four Young Girls

The beloved community would not arrive painlessly. Again, tragedy followed close upon the heels of triumph. On September 15, 1963, four hundred worshipers squeezed into Birmingham's Sixteenth

On September 22, 1963, the Congress of Racial Equality marched in Washington in memory of four young girls killed in Birmingham when a bomb was tossed into a crowded church.

Struck by an assassin's bullet, President John F. Kennedy (left of center) slumps forward in his limousine in Dallas, Texas. King saw the president's death as an omen of his own fate.

Street Baptist Church for Sunday service. Shortly before the service's start, someone tossed a bundle of dynamite through a window. In the ensuing explosion, four black girls were killed. Groups of angry blacks rioted in Birmingham's streets, during which two more blacks were killed.

King rushed to Birmingham that night to calm the situation and to vent his anger. In the eulogy he delivered for three of the girls, he forcefully asserted that one had to reach back to the days of Christians in the Roman catacombs to find such heinous attacks on churches. Few failed to notice that none of the city's white elected officials attended the funeral.

The Death of a President

Two months later, on November 22, 1963, King and his wife learned with the rest of the nation the shocking news that President John F. Kennedy had been assassinated in Dallas, Texas. While the news dismayed most of the nation, King somberly reflected on the event as a foreshadow of his death. Watching the events in Texas unfold on their television screen, King turned to Coretta and stated, "I don't think I'm going to live to reach forty." Coretta admonished him to stop such talk, but King added, "This is what is going to happen to me also. I keep

The Death of Kennedy

King issued a statement to reporters following President Kennedy's assassination. In their book King Remembered, *Flip Schulke and Penelope McPhee quote King's comments to the press.*

"While the question 'who killed President Kennedy?' is important, the question 'what killed him?' is more important. Our late president was assassinated by a morally inclement climate. It is a climate filled with heavy torrents of false accusation, jostling winds of hatred and raging storms of violence. It is a climate where men cannot disagree without being disagreeable, and where they express their dissent through violence and murder."

telling you, this is a sick nation. And I don't think I can survive either." [89]

He frequently faced the prospect that a bullet or bomb would cut his life short. Hardly a week passed that he did not receive a death threat, and some people wondered how he could function amid such hate and fear. One time, after learning that a racist military group led by a retired army officer had vowed to kill King if he stepped foot into Mississippi, King's aides begged him to stay away. King, who had planned to travel to the state, ignored their pleas:

If I were constantly worried about death, I couldn't function. After a while, if your life is more or less constantly in peril, you come to a point where you accept the possibility philosophically. I must face the fact, . . . that something could well happen to me at any time. I feel, though, that my cause is so right, so moral, that if I should lose my life, in some way it would aid the cause. [90]

Within three months of his heralded "I Have a Dream" speech, King bore the sad burden of eulogizing three little girls—killed by the racism he worked so hard to eradicate—and mourning for a president who held out hope to the civil rights movement. The beloved community of which James Baldwin spoke seemed even more distant.

Glimpses of hope flickered among the sorrow, however. In December 1963 Atlanta finally banned segregation in public facilities. Included in that was Funtown, the amusement park King's daughter so wanted to visit. Now legally open to them, King and his daughter wasted little time arranging their first outing.

The year ended with *Time* magazine honoring King as its "Man of the Year." The civil rights leader, the first black to be selected by *Time* for this award, had traveled 275,000 miles in 1963 and delivered 350 speeches, including his "I Have a Dream" oration at the Lincoln Memorial. This honor brought more attention to the plight of black people in the nation.

Violence in St. Augustine

In May 1964 the SCLC decided to campaign for equal rights in St. Augustine, Florida, the oldest established city in North America. They could hardly have chosen a more difficult target, for St. Augustine boasted a strong Ku Klux Klan organization that terrorized local blacks. In recent years Klan members had burned to death four blacks, had bombed numerous homes, and had boldly formed a "hunting club" whose purpose was to hunt "coons." When five black and two white civil rights workers attempted to integrate a local motel and dove into its pool, the manager dumped two jugs of hydrochloric acid into the water. Though gorgeous beaches stretched along the city's eastern end, blacks were warned to stay away.

One white resident, Holsted "Hoss" Manucy, bragged that the only vice he had was to "beat and kill niggers."[91] Everyone understood that campaigning in St. Augustine, a place King labeled as "one of the most segregated cities in America,"[92] might cause violence to erupt.

King sent his top assistants to start the activities. On May 28 Andrew Young led a group of blacks to St. Augustine's old slave market in the town's public square, where scores of waiting Klansmen attacked them with bicycle chains and iron pipes. Police, purposely moving slowly while the Klan beat Young and others, finally halted the violence.

Knights of the Ku Klux Klan burn a cross in Florida, where the Klan had a strong presence. They frequently terrorized blacks and civil rights workers with acts of violence and hostility.

King arrived three days later to begin negotiations with town leaders, who quickly rejected each demand. Meanwhile, blacks marched to the slave market or conducted "swim-ins" at the local beaches, while whites countered with their own rallies. Tension built as the opposing groups each asserted they would achieve victory.

One night King led a small line of marchers to a segregated motel. When a larger throng of hostile whites threatened to throw the marchers into the swimming pool, one of King's aides advised that they quickly leave, but King refused. As the whites shouted obscenities, King completed his march and led the blacks toward their cars. One marcher said later, "I was scared they were going to jump us. But King was so calm. His eyes—I don't know how to describe eyes like that. You could just look at them and think, well, if he can do it, somehow nothing will happen to me."[93]

On June 25 eight hundred Klansmen attacked another line of black marchers. They tore the clothes off a teenage girl, then beat a magazine reporter when he tried to help her escape. King feared that the situation had disintegrated; when he appealed to the federal government for assistance, President Lyndon Baines Johnson, who had succeeded the slain Kennedy, refused to dispatch federal marshals. When Florida's governor banned the SCLC's night marches while saying nothing about the Klan, King decided that the St. Augustine campaign had achieved all it could.

Before he departed, however, a biracial committee was set up to explore racial matters in the town. Though one SCLC leader stated that "St. Augustine was the toughest nut I have seen in all my days of working in cities in direct-action campaigns,"[94] King

had at least pursuaded white leaders to open talks with black residents.

Civil Rights and the Nobel Peace Prize

The latter half of 1964 brought bright moments for King. Following Kennedy's assassination support increased for a stronger civil rights bill. Finally, on July 2, President Johnson signed the Civil Rights Act, outlawing with a stroke of his pen segregation in public facilities and discrimination in the workplace, and approving the withholding of federal money from businesses that practiced discrimination. No longer would black men and women be forced to gaze at signs stating Whites Only. As the president said, "Those who are equal before God shall now be equal in the polling booths, in the classrooms, in the factories, and in hotels, restaurants, movie theaters, and other places that provide service to the public."[95] Though the law said nothing about fair housing, voting rights, or poverty, it was a significant step forward for civil rights.

Another step occurred in October, when the Norwegian Parliament awarded King the 1964 Nobel Peace Prize, given annually to the individual who helped achieve the greatest strides in world peace. At age thirty-five King was the youngest to receive the honor and only the third black—behind American Ralph Bunche and South Africa's chief Albert Luthuli— to be so honored.

He and Coretta traveled to Oslo for the ceremony. On December 10, with Norway's king Olav V watching, King received the award in the auditorium of

King Accepts the Nobel Peace Prize

King humbly accepted the Nobel Peace Prize in December 1964. Editor James Melvin Washington includes King's acceptance speech in his book A Testament of Hope: The Essential Writings and Speeches of Martin Luther King Jr.

"I believe that even amid today's mortar bursts and whining bullets, there is still hope for a brighter tomorrow. I believe that wounded justice, lying prostrate on the blood-flowing streets of our nations, can be lifted from this dust of shame to reign supreme among the children of men.

I have the audacity to believe that peoples everywhere can have three meals a day for their bodies, education and culture for their minds, and dignity, equality and freedom for their spirits."

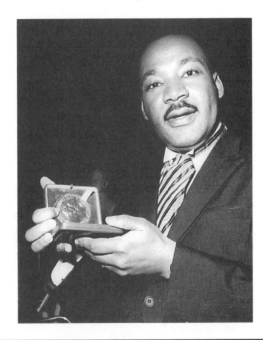

King displays his 1964 Nobel Peace Prize medal in Oslo, Norway.

Oslo University. In accepting it, King pointed out that much work remained to be done: "I accept the Nobel Prize for Peace at a moment when twenty-two million Negroes of the United States are engaged in a creative battle to end the long night of racial injustice." He added that "I am mindful that only yesterday in Birmingham, Alabama, our children, crying out for brotherhood, were answered with fire hoses, snarling dogs, and even death."[96] King donated the monetary portion of the award—$54,600—to various civil rights organizations.

King returned to the United States to widespread acclaim. Even a few southern voices publicly proclaimed his value to the nation. Liberal newspaper reporter Ralph McGill of the Atlanta *Constitution* wrote that "the South one day will be grateful when it realizes what the alternative would have been had Dr. King, with his capacity to stir and inspire, come preaching violence, hate and aggression."[97]

For every supporter—black and white—King knew that many more opposed him in his uphill struggle to wrest dignity and equality for all black people. In a sermon to a gathering in a New York City church shortly after crossing the ocean from Norway, King referred to this fight and his own exhaustion: "I have been to the mountaintop. I really wish I could stay on the mountain; but I must go back to the valley. I must go back, because my brothers and sisters down in Mississippi and Alabama are sweltering under the heat of injustice."[98]

Hoover and the FBI

The heat of injustice plagued King more than most people realized. King created enemies with his insistence that the black community be given its fair share, and one of his most staunch opponents possessed enormous governmental power. J. Edgar Hoover, for years the bigoted head of the Federal Bureau of Investigation (FBI), hated King and used his agency in repeated attempts to ruin King's reputation.

Hoover Targets King

In his book They Had a Dream: The Civil Rights Struggle, *Jules Archer describes J. Edgar Hoover's initial interest in stopping King.*

"Martin's swift rise to prominence as a black leader determined to challenge Jim Crow laws aroused the hostility of FBI chief J. Edgar Hoover, the racist who targeted Marcus Garvey [a civil rights leader before King's era] for prosecution. Hoover now ordered Martin placed under secret surveillance as a 'Communist.'

In 1956 Hoover initiated a program called COINTELPRO. Its operations included infiltration of suspect civil rights and liberal groups, disruption of their activities, and propaganda designed to destroy their credibility. One of Hoover's objectives was to prevent the rise of a 'black messiah' who could 'unify and electrify a coalition of militant black nationalist groups.'

There was no doubt his target was Martin Luther King, Jr."

Hoping to uncover evidence that King was a Communist, as early as 1958 Hoover ordered FBI agents to follow King and to record his telephone conversations.

By 1963 Hoover's men had placed taps on every phone in King's home, at work, and in most hotels and motels in which King stayed while traveling. Though they found no material connecting King to the Communist Party, they did learn of the civil rights leader's frequent affairs. Hoover intended to use this sensational information to destroy King.

King suffered tremendous guilt over the affairs and tried to remain faithful to Coretta, but the temptations of frequently being on the road proved more than he could control. King knew he opened himself to heavy criticism by engaging in this activity, but he never imagined that someone as powerful as Hoover would so closely scrutinize his every move.

Hoover, who ranted to subordinates that King was one of the most immoral individuals in the country, handed sympathetic congressmen copies of a secret file labeled "Martin Luther King, Jr.: His Personal Conduct." No rumor was too unbelievable, no secondhand source of information too unreliable for Hoover to ignore. Everything became grist for his mill.

In late 1964 King received a package in the mail containing a tape recording of some of his after-hours meetings with females. Along with it was an unsigned letter warning, "King, there is only one thing left for you to do. . . . You are done. There is but one way out for you. You better take it before your filthy, abnormal fraudulent self is bared to the nation."[99] This blatant

William C. Sullivan, J. Edgar Hoover's chief assistant at the FBI, attempted to blackmail King with recordings made of the reverend's marital unfaithfulness.

attempt to convince King to commit suicide was sent by William C. Sullivan, Hoover's chief assistant at the FBI. King admitted to Coretta that the voice was his, but he stated that he would not permit Hoover to blackmail him.

Though the two men met in December 1964, nothing changed. FBI agents continued to tap King's telephones, but King tried to ignore it so he could focus on his work. At times the situation dissolved into a comical game of trying to outwit the other side, with King and his aides checking into one hotel room, then hastily switching to another. As they chatted on the telephone, King and his advisers often added comments intended for the FBI agents they knew would be eavesdropping. One time King even sauntered up to some FBI agents who had been trailing him and said, "Hello, I'm Martin Luther King. I want to thank you for your 'protection.'"[100]

7 "I Wept Within That Night"

Now that the Civil Rights Act had been signed, King turned to discrimination at the voting booth. Blacks would never achieve lasting gains until they proved to the nation's elected officials that they were a force that could only be ignored at peril of losing the next election. When King examined southern voting patterns, he saw a dismal image—in many locations whites prevented blacks from voting through intimidation and threat. The Ku Klux Klan issued warnings in some instances. Elsewhere, city ordinances forced blacks to take a difficult literacy test that asked them to recite, word for word, the preamble to the Constitution.

Black voters are forced to wait outside in the rain for their turn at the ballot box in Selma, Alabama. Such tactics kept black registration and participation in southern elections at intolerably low levels.

Sheriff Jim Clark waves a billy club as he orders black voters to leave the county courthouse in Selma. When they refused he arrested more than one hundred people.

Consequently, the number of black voters was pitifully small. Only 6 percent of Mississippi blacks had registered to vote by 1960. In two Alabama counties, though blacks comprised 80 percent of the population, only one individual was registered. Fear and violence kept the others away.

Selma and Jim Clark

King selected Selma, Alabama, in Dallas County as the site for his voter registration campaign. Of 15,000 eligible blacks, only 383 had registered. Besides, the county contained the perfect adversary for King and his marchers, who hoped to find an-

other Bull Connor. Hard-nosed sheriff Jim Clark loved to saunter about with his billy club and electric cattle prod and boast that he would preserve the white way of life.

Clark ruled the county with such an iron fist that black citizens feared walking about in any size group, even one as small as three or four. Hosea Williams, an SCLC official, claimed that "anytime four or more people get together, they are arrested. Jim Clark even sent deputies into churches where people would be having worship service, to see whether they were serving God or whether they were talking civil rights." One of King's closest associates, Andrew Young, stated that "Selma was kind of like South Africa."[101]

On January 18, 1965, King led the first march to the county courthouse to register

On March 21, 1965, Martin Luther King organized a march from Selma to Montgomery to present Alabama governor George C. Wallace (pictured) with a list of grievances. Wallace would not meet with him.

black citizens. Clark surprised everyone by reacting calmly, but two days later he vented his hate during another march by manhandling a black businesswoman and ordering sixty arrests. As King expected, news photographers and cameras recorded the hostile reaction.

When King conducted another march on February 1, Clark had him thrown into jail. Since King remained in custody for five days, the incident brought widespread news coverage to Selma and nationwide attention to voter discrimination.

One man who normally operated at odds with King in civil rights—Malcolm X—journeyed to Selma while King languished in jail. Malcolm X favored a more violent, noncompromising position than King, but on this occasion he tried to help

a fellow crusader. He explained to Coretta that he had not traveled to Selma to criticize King but to assist him: "If the white people realize what the alternative is [Malcolm X's violent approach], perhaps they will be more willing to hear Dr. King."[102] Unfortunately, the two civil rights leaders never received the chance to mend fences. Less than three weeks later, Malcolm X was gunned down in New York.

Shortly after King was released from jail on February 6, Sheriff Clark shocked onlookers with his brutal treatment of 165 black student marchers. After arresting them, Clark forced the students to run six miles to a lockup. Along the way his men jolted them with cattle prods and smacked them with clubs, causing many to bend over in pain or collapse in agony. Rather than incarcerate the entire lot, Clark allowed them to hobble away.

They were not the only ones to suffer. On February 18 state troopers attacked a group of marchers. In the melee, twenty-six-year-old Jimmy Lee Jackson rushed to protect his mother and grandmother but fell before he reached them, dropped by a gun blast to his stomach from a state trooper. The man was rushed to a hospital, where the head of the state police amazingly charged him with assault and battery. A few days later Jackson died in the hospital.

Bloody Sunday

To dramatize the plight of black voters, a huge march was planned for March 7. During the march King would lead walkers fifty miles from Selma to Montgomery to present a list of grievances to the state's governor, George C. Wallace. When the day arrived, though, King remained in Atlanta because he assumed everyone would be arrested before the march began.

Hosea Williams of the SCLC and John Lewis of SNCC filled in for King. As they walked through Selma, approaching the Edmund Pettis Bridge that traversed the Alabama River, the marchers spotted Sheriff Clark and a long line of state police stationed at the bridge's far end. One marcher recalled that "we saw a sea of blue—blue uniforms, blue helmets and patrol cars."

King and Malcolm X

King's nonviolent approach did not meet with approval from all civil rights leaders. In his biography Malcolm X: By Any Means Necessary, *Walter Dean Myers explains the differences between King and Malcolm X.*

"For all his public life Malcolm was compared to Martin Luther King, Jr. It was a comparison that Malcolm accepted, for it pointed out the differences between the Nation of Islam [Malcolm's group] and the traditional black protest movement that King represented. Dr. King urged blacks to maintain their own humanity in the face of white oppression, to love whites as brothers, despite discrimination and violence.

Malcolm said it was ridiculous for black men to 'turn the other cheek' when their women and children were being beaten and killed. Hostility was the only language, he said, that some people understood."

Though Malcolm X (pictured) and Martin Luther King were fighting for the same cause, their philosophies differed considerably. Malcolm X did not believe that pacifism was always the best way to achieve equality.

As Williams and Lewis started across the bridge, an officer shouted into a bullhorn for them to disperse. Williams asked the commanding officer of the state police if they could continue but received only the curt reply, "There's not going to be any talking today. You're going to take those niggers back to that church."

When the marchers knelt down on the bridge in silent protest, state police officers and Clark's deputies charged in, some using whips and rubber tubing wrapped with barbed wire. Clubs fractured skulls, nightsticks whacked arms and legs, whips lashed skin, and tear gas stung eyes. Lewis, who suffered a fractured skull, claimed "it was like a battle zone: all those people choking in the gas, being hit and beaten." People retreated from the bridge, gasping for air and vomiting from the gas. A woman pled "Please, no! God, we're being killed." [103] Almost eighty people had to be treated for broken bones, cracked heads, and cuts.

The day called "Bloody Sunday" stunned King, who felt guilty for remaining in Atlanta. He immediately issued a call to ministers around the nation to join him in Selma for a gigantic protest march on Tuesday, March 9.

Four hundred leaders from all faiths joined one thousand other marchers on that day. Though a judge had issued an injunction forbidding the activity and government officials begged him to cancel because they feared the violence that might erupt, King would not be deterred. He stated that he would rather die than betray his conscience.

King led the group to the Edmund Pettis Bridge, where again a line of club-wielding police waited on the other side. He cautiously guided the marchers across to the Jefferson Davis Highway and asked police officials if he could lead his people in prayer. When the prayer was completed and the group had sung "We Shall Overcome," the police opened a path for the marchers instead of arresting them, as King had expected. Suspicious that a trap had been set and that he might be leading the group to beatings and even death, King reversed course and took the marchers back to the church. King did not realize that Governor Wallace issued strict orders to Clark to avoid a repeat of Bloody Sunday.

Immediately, civil rights activists from SNCC criticized King as a coward for passively pulling back. The ranks of those who favored a more confrontational approach to achieving equality had been increasing as days and months passed without significant gains, and they were willing to use violence to attain their goals. Angered over King's tactics, SNCC pulled out of the Selma campaign, creating a rift in the civil rights movement.

Troubling Events

The next day emotions intensified when a white Unitarian minister from Boston, James J. Reeb, who had traveled to Selma to support King, was attacked by four whites. Shouting, "You want to know what it's like to be a real nigger?" [104] the whites viciously attacked Reeb and two companions with clubs. The Boston minister slumped to the sidewalk with a crushed skull and died two days later.

The incident produced a huge outcry around the country. Disturbed by the events in Selma, on March 15 President

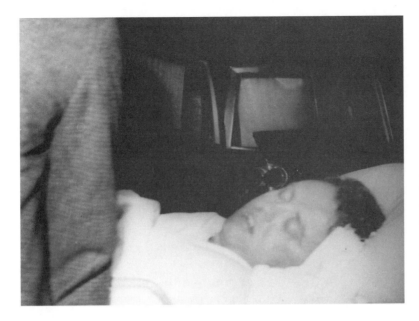

Reverend James J. Reeb lies unconscious in an ambulance after he was beaten by four white men during a rally held in Selma. His death two days later sparked President Johnson to ask Congress for a strong voters' rights bill.

Johnson delivered a nationally televised address before Congress in which he requested a strong voting rights bill.

Though pleased with Johnson's firm stand, civil rights activists could not fail to notice that the president acted only after a white minister had been killed. Johnson sent flowers to Mrs. Reeb and mentioned the incident in his speech, but when Jimmy Lee Jackson, a black man, had been killed earlier in the campaign, he had been silent.

An Atlanta event occurring about the same time emphasized how far King still had to go in his quest for equality. The integrated school that his oldest son and daughter attended staged a musical performance highlighting great music from immigrant groups. As King later explained, he and Coretta "were certain that the program would end with the most original of all American music, the Negro spiritual. But we were mistaken. Instead, all the students, including our children, ended the program by singing 'Dixie.'"

The two parents were shocked to listen to their son and daughter singing the rallying song for Confederate forces in the Civil War, and they were saddened that not one contribution from black America appeared in the program. "I wept within that night," King wrote. "I wept for my children and all black children who have been denied a knowledge of their heritage; I wept for all white children, who, through daily miseducation, are taught that the Negro is an irrelevant entity in American society."[105]

March to Montgomery

On March 21 King commenced a ninety-mile march to the state capitol in Montgomery, where he intended to hand a list of grievances to Governor Wallace. The governor declared that such a lengthy demonstration would disrupt traffic and endanger many lives, so he ordered the Alabama state police to employ any means necessary to stop King.

To prevent violence, President Johnson assumed control of the Alabama National Guard and posted them along the intended route. With this personal guarantee of safety, King led thirty-two hundred marchers out of Selma toward Montgomery. Crowds of jeering whites lined the highways, but the National Guard prevented any from attacking the marchers.

Once the throng of civil rights workers reached Lowndes County, all but three hundred specially chosen Freedom Marchers dwindled away. The smaller group, including Rosa Parks, then walked the remaining miles into Montgomery, past Dexter Avenue Baptist Church where King had started his career, and to the capitol, where Jefferson Davis had once labored to maintain slavery.

Though Governor Wallace refused to meet with King, the Selma campaign succeeded in placing southern bigotry before the nation and the world. Once again a sheriff's violent tactics played into King's hands and showcased for an appalled audience what blacks experienced in the South. John Lewis claimed that Selma was "the high point of the civil rights movement. After Selma, the South and the American political system were never the same again."[106]

As a result, President Johnson and Congress moved swiftly to pass a voting rights bill. On August 6, 1965, with King standing behind him, Johnson signed the Voting Rights Act. Henceforward, literacy tests or any other manner of voting restrictions were forbidden, and the attorney general received power to supervise federal elections to ensure fairness.

With the new safeguards to ensure their voting privileges, southern blacks

---

"Who Is Their God?"

King later admitted that one of the biggest mistakes he made was to assume that white southern ministers would help his cause. He never could comprehend such an attitude from men of God, as he explained in a 1965 magazine interview, excerpted in editor James Melvin Washington's A Testament of Hope.

"I ended up, of course, chastened and disillusioned. As our movement unfolded, and direct appeals were made to white ministers, most folded their hands—and some even took stands *against* us. . . . Time and again in my travels, as I have seen the outward beauty of white churches, I have had to ask myself, 'What kind of people worship there? Who is their God? Is their God the God of Abraham, Isaac and Jacob, and is their Savior the Savior who hung on the cross at Golgotha? Where were their voices when a black race took upon itself the cross of protest against man's injustice to man? Where were their voices when defiance and hatred were called for by white men who sat in these very churches?'"

President Lyndon Johnson presents King with a pen used to sign the Voting Rights Act. Though pleased with the new legislation, King wondered why it took the death of a white minister to get a tough response from the White House.

registered in tremendous numbers. They quickly made their presence known in the 1966 elections, in which fifty-two black candidates filed for office in Alabama alone, with four winning. Voters tossed Sheriff Clark out of office, and within a few years even Selma contained a racially mixed city council.

Criticism from All Sides

King had struggled on the national scene for a decade, yet he still sometimes felt that he hammered at an immovable object. He continued to believe that nonvio-

lent methods would achieve true gains, but others in civil rights doubted their effectiveness. As a result, King had to answer critics from both white opponents, who contended King asked for too much, and from black leaders, who argued that King asked for too little.

To those who claimed that blacks pushed for too much, a frustrated King replied, "Why do white people seem to find it so difficult to understand that the Negro is sick and tired of having reluctantly parceled out to him those rights and privileges which all others receive upon birth or entry in America?"[107] As for those black leaders who thought King had become too conservative—they had even

Some civil rights activists like Stokely Carmichael (pictured) began to wonder if King's time had passed. They favored more radical approaches to fighting racism as opposed to King's methods of civil disobedience.

begun calling King "de Lawd"—he wondered if they were jealous that he received so much world attention.

Some blacks favored a more confrontational manner of correcting society's ills, particularly Stokely Carmichael of SNCC, who preferred to use the term Afro-American instead of Negro and to espouse what he called Black Power. Some thought that King's time had passed, that he no longer could be an effective civil rights leader in a time of increasing anger and violence. "If every Negro in the United States turns to violence," stated King, "I will choose to be that one lone voice preaching that this is the wrong voice." [108]

As proof that nonviolence worked, King cited a number of achievements in the past ten years, including the Montgomery bus boycott, successful sit-ins, the Freedom Riders, Birmingham, and Selma. "Fewer people have been killed in ten years of nonviolent demonstrations across the South than were killed in one night of rioting in Watts," [109] he countered. He would not abandon his approach, but the backbiting must have made him yearn even more for the time when he could qui-

etly teach, read, and contemplate theology in a peaceful university setting.

Watts and Other Big Cities

The riot mentioned by King occurred in the summer of 1965. An impoverished section of Los Angeles inhabited by the city's black population, Watts was the scene of violence and looting that ended with thirty-four killed, nine hundred injured, and $46 million worth of property destroyed. When King toured the area in the action's aftermath, young blacks, many of whom participated in the looting and destruction, claimed they had won. King asked how they could make this claim when much of their own community had been demolished. One young black person answered, "We won because we made the whole world pay attention to us." [110]

King knew he had to achieve further gains with nonviolence so that blacks would not resort to bloodshed. He turned to large northern cities, where blacks who lived amid poverty, slums, and crime appeared

Big Cities in Turmoil

The eruptions that occurred in many American cities put the nation on notice that it must take action to prevent worse rioting. In her history of the civil rights movement Tear Down the Walls!, *Dorothy Sterling quotes a resident of Watts.*

"'For years we've been trying to get the mayor to come out and talk to us but he wouldn't come,' a man said after the explosion in Watts in which thirty-four people—thirty of them Negroes—lost their lives and forty million dollars' worth of property was destroyed. 'For years we tried to get the governor but he wouldn't come. For years we tried to get all those white folks downtown to come and pay some attention to us. But after we burned, baby, the whole world came to look at us.'"

A National Guard jeep patrols Watts, an area in Los Angeles where heavy rioting broke out in the summer of 1965.

ready to explode in anger. In early 1966 he selected Chicago, Illinois, as his target. One million blacks lived in the Chicago area, mainly confined to ghettos on the city's south and west sides by real estate practices that kept blacks out of all-white neighborhoods. As a result schoolchildren attended largely all-black schools.

In choosing Chicago, King placed himself against a formidable foe—Chicago's Mayor Richard Daley, whose political machine dominated area politics. To gain black votes, Daley offered jobs in his machine and periodically cited for code violations owners of black slum buildings. Like mayors of most northern cities, Daley supported King when he marched on southern locales, but reacted with disgust when King turned his gaze toward northern slums.

On January 26, 1966, King and his wife moved into a shabby apartment in Chicago's "Slumdale." The building smelled of urine from drunks who relieved themselves in its hallways, and King's dingy apartment contained an unusable refrigerator and heaters that did little to fight off Chicago's blustery cold. As soon as the landlord realized who had moved in, however, he dispatched a work crew to clean up the apartment, replace broken-down appliances, and apply a fresh coat of paint. The *Chicago Sun-Times* joked that if King gradually moved from block to block, he would eliminate all of the city's slums.

Though King was on the road during much of the next six months, he and Coretta called Slumdale their home. While he traveled about the nation giving speeches, King's main assistants organized Chicago demonstrations in hopes of attaining change.

Not much had been accomplished by July 12, a scorching summer day. To escape the day's heat, black youths turned on a number of fire hydrants in their neighborhood, but when police arrived to turn off the hydrants, violence flared. Two days later worse violence erupted when police and black snipers engaged in a gunfight. By day's end two people had been killed and fifty-six injured, prodding Illinois's governor to send four thousand National Guardsmen to control the chaos in Chicago.

In reaction, King organized a series of marches into all-white neighborhoods near the end of July and first part of August. The reaction from white Chicago surpassed any that King had encountered in Alabama or Mississippi. During one march whites hurled rocks and bottles at Chicago civil rights activist Jesse Jackson, and dur-

Though he publicly supported King when his marches were aimed at southern racism, Chicago mayor Richard Daley (pictured) reacted with anger when King turned his attention toward his city.

ing another a rock hit King in the head with so much force that he slumped to his knees. While some defiant whites threatened King to leave town and threw debris at the demonstrators, including a knife that barely missed King, others proudly displayed Confederate flags and Nazi insignias. "I worked all my life for a house out here," asserted one elderly white citizen, "and no nigger is going to get it!"[111]

King had expected bitterness in the Deep South, but the hostility from Chicago's white neighborhoods stunned him. "I've been in many demonstrations all across the South, but I can say that I have never seen—even in Mississippi and Alabama—mobs as hostile and as hate-filled as I've seen in Chicago,"[112] he sadly concluded.

He would not stop, however. When some wondered why he kept marching in such an unfriendly environment, King answered, "You want us to stop marching, make justice a reality. I don't mind saying to Chicago—or to anybody—I'm tired of marching. I'm tired of marching for something that should have been mine at birth."[113]

Mayor Daley, under increasing criticism for the violence, met with King after the civil rights leader scheduled a demonstration into the wealthy, all-white suburb of Cicero, where there was sure to be an unfriendly reception. On August 26 Daley agreed to work toward integration of all neighborhoods and to encourage banks to lend money to black families so they could purchase decent homes. While some praised the outcome in Chicago, others refused to trust Daley. Sadly, the skeptics proved correct, for once King and his civil rights marchers left Illinois, Daley took no further action in this area.

Though King had at least implemented the groundwork for future civil rights work by Chicago, he was disappointed in the outcome; it caused him to believe that most whites, in both the North and the South, opposed integration. Their intransigence at giving blacks a fair shake caused frustrated blacks to resort to violence. As King explains, "At least in the South, the Negro can see pockets of progress, but this isn't true of the Negro in the northern ghetto"[114] who lived in rat-infested slums that only worsened by the year. When rioting tore apart places like Detroit, Milwaukee, and Cincinnati the following summer, King wondered if his nonviolent approach would ever attain equality.

James Meredith

King's doubts intensified during an incident in Mississippi. On June 6, 1966, James Meredith, the first black student admitted to the University of Mississippi, was shot by a white man as he embarked on a one-man walk from Memphis, Tennessee, to Jackson, Mississippi, in an attempt to increase voter registration in that state. King immediately stepped in for the injured Meredith and completed the march, but disturbances both along the route and within civil rights ranks hounded him. In one Mississippi Klan stronghold, whites lobbed cherry bombs toward the demonstrators and shot at their camp at night. On June 23 a line of state and local police attacked King and the other marchers with tear gas and clubs.

Violence was nothing new or surprising to King, however. What bothered him more was the internal strife that simmered each day as the marchers advanced toward

James Meredith (center), the first black student to attend class at the University of Mississippi, was shot while trying to increase voter registration in that state.

Jackson. Stokely Carmichael, the chairman of SNCC, and Floyd McKissick, head of the Congress of Racial Equality (CORE), criticized King for being too cautious in his demands. These men and their followers contended that a more aggressive, noncompromising position would produce greater results from an unyielding white majority.

Consequently, the younger black activists were more willing to use violence if any trouble flared. One militant claimed, "I'm not for that nonviolence stuff anymore. If one of these damn Mississippi crackers touches me, I'm gonna knock the hell out of him." Frequent cries of "Black Power!" disrupted the march, and Carmichael disdained help from white civil rights workers. "We don't need any more white phonies and liberals invading our movement,"[115] he warned.

These sentiments disturbed King, who felt they conveyed the notion that blacks were better than whites. He saw little difference in this attitude and the bigoted belief that a white was better than a black, which was what they all opposed. He spoke with Carmichael, and while the younger compatriot agreed not to disrupt any of King's rallies, he refused to change his stance toward violence.

King and the others completed the walk to Jackson, but a disheartened leader returned to Atlanta. Instead of displaying unity, the Mississippi march showed that serious divisions existed in the civil rights movement. It seemed that everywhere he turned, King ran into the Black Power slogan. Hoping to mend the rift and to unite the nation in a new campaign, King instituted plans for the nation's poor—black and white—to gather in Washington, D.C., for a nonviolent rally to bring attention to poverty. Maybe in that manner he could reunite black leaders and bring blacks and whites together in a common cause.

8 "Free at Last"

King worried that the civil rights movement was spinning out of his control and into the hands of those who favored a militant approach. He warned audiences that "today the choice is no longer between violence and nonviolence. It is either nonviolence or nonexistence."[116] In 1967 he attacked another event whose presence further endangered world peace—the expanding conflict in Vietnam. In the process King alienated more people and set himself up as a target for criticism—and worse.

The Vietnam War

Vietnam rested on the other side of the world. Directly south of China, Vietnamese Communist forces under their national leader Ho Chi Minh battled first the French, and then the United States, in an effort to gain independence. President Johnson, determined to stop what he saw as a worldwide conspiracy to spread communism, committed increasing numbers of soldiers to the fight. King believed that the Vietnamese were more concerned with gaining independence than they were with installing a Communist government; thus he contended that the United States had

In 1967 King turned his attention to criticizing the escalating U.S. involvement in Vietnam, where blacks bore the brunt of the fighting. He also recognized that the cost of the war was diverting money from civil rights and antipoverty programs at home.

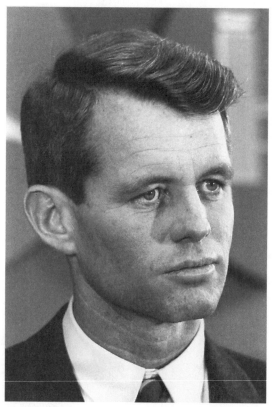

Robert Kennedy was one of the few prominent Americans who, along with King and a small handful of senators, opposed the American military presence in Vietnam.

He told audiences, "I knew that America would never invest the necessary funds or energies in rehabilitation of its poor so long as adventures like Vietnam continued to draw men and skills and money like some demoniacal destructive suction tube." He pointed to the astonishing irony that the United States supposedly sent soldiers around the world to guarantee the rights of a foreign nation while it denied those same rights to its own citizens: "We were taking the black young men who had been crippled by our society and sending them 8,000 miles away to guarantee liberties in Southeast Asia which they had not found in Southwest Georgia and East Harlem."[117]

King joined a small group of anti–Vietnam War protesters, which included Robert Kennedy and Senator William Fulbright of Arkansas, in attacking a war that most people at that time favored. The *New York Times* blasted King's stance, and even black colleagues such as Ralph Bunche, Whitney Young, and Jackie Robinson criticized King's views. Many Americans called King a traitor, and an irate President Johnson, who thought he had aided the civil rights movement with a series of legislation, believed that King had ungraciously turned on him. As a result, Hoover's FBI kept an even closer watch on King.

Death Threats

In the center of more turmoil, King fretted over the alarming rise in death threats—the FBI knew of fifty assassination threats against King. In the St. Louis area, a right-wing white businessman named John Kauffmann quietly circulated an offer of thirty thousand dollars to anyone who

no right to intrude into their affairs. When he realized how much the war effort detracted from civil rights and antipoverty programs, King decided to speak out.

Though his trusted aides, fearing a savage backlash, tried to pursuade him to remain silent on the war, King delivered his first anti-Vietnam speech on February 25, 1967. Over the following weeks and months he emphasized the same points—the United States had no right becoming involved in another nation's affairs, the war diverted sorely needed funds from antipoverty programs, and too many young men died in a useless cause.

killed "the big nigger," and attorney John Sutherland offered fifty thousand dollars. Though certain that he was stalked at every moment, King refused to let any of his assistants carry weapons, claiming, "If a man has not found something worth giving his life for, he is not fit to live."[118]

The inordinate strain of trying to mend a civil rights rift, taking an unpopular stance against the Vietnam War, and death threats took a heavy toll on King. As Ralph Abernathy recalls, King "was nervous, very, very jittery."[119] On a plane trip in February 1968 King even delivered what he thought would be a fitting eulogy for himself and started telling Abernathy what to do with the SCLC after his death. The talk alarmed his close friend, but Abernathy could do little to stop it.

To Memphis

King's attention turned to Memphis, Tennessee, where black garbage collectors were striking in February 1968 to protest poor wages and unfair practices. The strikers asked King to come to Memphis to speak and lend support.

On March 28 King and Abernathy led the striking garbage collectors in a march.

Martin Luther King and Ralph Abernathy lead a march in support of black garbage collectors on strike in Memphis, Tennessee. The rally was marred by vandalism and acts of outrage.

The marchers walked arm-in-arm and sang "We Shall Overcome"; before they had advanced three blocks, however, loud noises from the rear of the line interrupted the singing.

"What was that?" King asked Abernathy. When he learned that young blacks had started throwing rocks and destroying property, he quickly called off the march in hopes of avoiding further harm. Afraid that King might be injured, one of his aides, Bernard Lee, halted a car driven by a black woman and asked if she would drive them out of the area. They headed

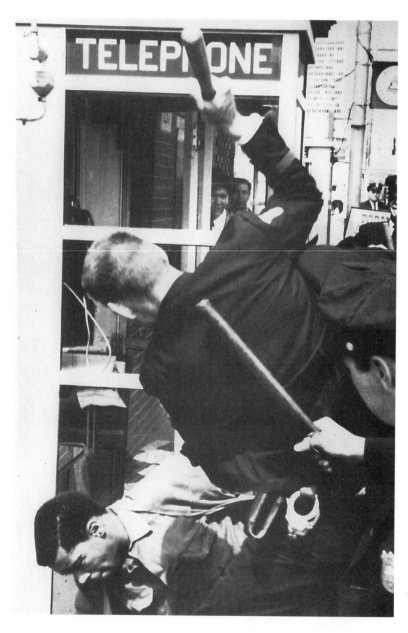

A demonstrator is beaten to the ground by a police officer during the violence that stemmed from the garbage collectors strike in Memphis. King had called off the first march because black youths began destroying property.

toward a police officer to enlist his help, then drove out of danger.

The day of violence dismayed King. When the governor declared a state of emergency in Memphis and ordered in the National Guard, a forlorn King mentioned to Abernathy that maybe the advocates of violence were gaining momentum. Abernathy later claimed that he had never seen his friend so depressed. Unable to sleep, King fretted that the violent outburst would hamper his plans for the Poor People's Campaign in Washington, D.C., and decided that he had to lead a peaceful march in Memphis to repair the harm. He made plans to return in early April for another attempt.

and mentioned how close to death he had been when the lady stabbed him in New York City. He talked about the numerous death threats he had received. In a quiet, halting manner, he told the crowd, "Like anybody, I would like to live a long life. Longevity has its place. But I'm not concerned about that now. I just want to do God's will. And He's allowed me to go up to the mountain. And I've looked over, and I've seen the promised land."

He then uttered the words that some later claimed indicated King had a premonition of the next day's events. "I may not get there with you, but I want you to know tonight that we as a people will get to the promised land."[121]

April 3, 1968

If the morning of April 3 were an omen, the following days would not be banner ones. King and Abernathy boarded an airplane in Atlanta bound for Memphis, but before they had a chance to settle comfortably into their seats, the pilot made an announcement: "We're sorry for the delay. But we have Dr. Martin Luther King on the plane. And to be sure that all the bags were checked and to be sure that nothing would be wrong in the plane, we had to check out everything carefully."[120] The airport had received a bomb threat, and authorities were taking nothing for granted.

The flight landed in Memphis without further mishap, but the incident, combined with the other turmoil swirling about King and the civil rights movement, put King in a melancholy mood. That night he delivered a speech in Memphis

April 4, 1968

The next day proved as hectic as any other, with King immersed in meetings, telephone calls, and chats with a variety of individuals. Around 4:00 P.M. he and Abernathy met in A. D. King's room at the Lorraine Motel for an hour of friendly conversation, then ambled to their own rooms to get dressed for dinner at a local minister's home.

At 5:30 King asked Abernathy if he was ready, but Abernathy replied that he needed to return to his room for some aftershave lotion. "OK," said King. "I'll be standing out here on the balcony." As Abernathy briefly disappeared into his room, King walked outside into the cool April evening and stepped to the iron railing along the balcony. Sighting Jesse Jackson, he invited the Chicago activist to dinner: "And you be sure to dress up a little tonight, OK, Jesse? No blue jeans, all right?"

Martin Luther King stands with Jesse Jackson and Ralph Abernathy on the balcony of the Lorraine Motel in Memphis seconds before King was struck by an assassin's bullet.

At that very moment an assailant was aiming his powerful rifle at King's head. James Earl Ray, a member of the right-wing American Independent Party, stood in an empty bathtub in a room across from the Lorraine Motel, peered through an open window, and fired. People near King heard a loud crack. King muttered, "Oh . . ."[122] and slumped to the ground. The bullet had torn off King's necktie, severed vital arteries leading to his heart, and fractured his spine in several places. Virtually the entire right side of his jaw and neck was gone.

"Take cover!" yelled one of the aides. Aghast, Abernathy rushed over to tend to the fallen King, moaning, "Oh my God, Martin's been shot." Another individual

grabbed a towel and placed it on King's neck to stem the gushing blood. "Martin, this is me, this is Ralph, this is Ralph," shouted Abernathy. "Don't be afraid." When another aide spotted particles of King's flesh splattered on the balcony's ceiling, he thought, "He's dead. He's really dead."

An ambulance quickly arrived and sped King to a nearby hospital, where physicians cut away King's coat and shirt to examine the wounds. When Abernathy saw a grapefruit-sized hole in King's body, he realized that little could be done to save his friend. Doctors concluded the same. One doctor mentioned to Abernathy that, if by some miracle King survived, "he will be a vegetable for the rest of his life, for he will be paralyzed from the neck down." Moments later, at 7:05 P.M., King died.

Abernathy and another aide, Bernard Lee, removed King's personal effects from the body. Lee dwelt on all the exhausting endeavors that occupied King and thought, "I know he was tired. Now maybe he'll get some rest."[123] Abernathy then composed himself and left the emergency room to speak to a throng of reporters.

In Atlanta, Coretta King learned of the tragedy and hurried to the airport along with the city's mayor, Ivan Allen Jr., and his wife. While waiting at the airport, Allen received news that King had died and spoke to Coretta: "Mrs. King, I have to inform you that Dr. King is dead." When he asked if she wanted to continue to Memphis, she answered that she preferred returning home to be with the children. When she walked through the front door, seven-year-old Dexter asked, "Mommy, when is Daddy coming home?"[124] Coretta gathered her children around her, quietly explained what had happened to their father, then disappeared into a bedroom for a few moments of solitary grieving.

Twelve-year-old Yolanda struggled with the news, not wanting to believe what her mother had said. After fifteen minutes, though, she regained composure, because "it kind of dawned on me that Daddy always said to us it can happen, so you've got to be prepared."[125]

"All of It Was Gone"

King's parents heard the news over the radio. Daddy later recalled, "My first son, whose birth had brought me such joy that I jumped up in the hall outside the

Robert Kennedy Speaks

Shortly before delivering a speech in Indianapolis, Robert Kennedy learned of King's death. In her history of the United States All the People, *Joy Hakim quotes Kennedy's words that day.*

"Martin Luther King dedicated his life to love and to justice for his fellow human beings, and he died because of that effort. In this difficult day, in this difficult time for the United States, it is perhaps well to ask what kind of nation we are and what direction we want to move in. . . . you can be filled with bitterness, with hatred, and a desire for revenge. We can move in that direction as a country. . . .

Or we can make an effort, as Martin Luther King did, to understand and to comprehend, and to replace that violence, that stain of bloodshed that has spread across our land, with an effort to understand with compassion and love."

room where he was born and touched the ceiling—the child, the scholar, the preacher . . . all of it was gone."[126] Elsewhere, staff members of the Ebenezer Baptist Church walked like zombies, too stunned to speak. As Daddy King recalled, "Ebenezer was so quiet; all through the church, as the staff learned what had happened, the tears flowed, but almost completely in silence."[127]

Words of praise and sympathy poured in from around the nation. The *New York Times* declared that the country would sorely miss King, a man of "integrity, vision and restraint."[128] President Johnson called Coretta King to offer condolences, dispatched Attorney General Ramsey Clark to take charge of the investigation in Memphis, and declared April 7 as a national day of mourning.

Unfortunately, the killing of Martin Luther King Jr.—a man who advocated nonviolence with every breath—also produced a wave of violence across the United States. Rioting engulfed more than one hundred cities, causing thirty-nine deaths and $45 million worth of damage. To maintain order, twenty thousand regular army troops and fifteen thousand National Guard forces were deployed to Washington, D.C., Chicago, and Baltimore. Fully armed soldiers guarded the White House, and a machine-gun crew protected the Capitol.

The next day Stokely Carmichael bluntly warned America that it could not expect another calm leader like King to take his place:

> When white America killed Dr. King last night she declared war on us. It would have been better if she had killed Rap Brown [another militant black leader] . . . or Stokely Carmichael. But when she killed Dr. King, she lost it. . . . He was the one man in our race who was trying to teach our people to have love, compassion, and mercy for white people.

Carmichael urged blacks to get their guns, and when a reporter asked if he feared for his life, Carmichael replied, "The hell with my life. You should fear for yours. I know I'm going to die."[129]

On Monday, April 8, Coretta King and her three older children led a memorial

Rosa Parks Learns of the Shooting

In her autobiography Rosa Parks: My Story, *Parks recalls hearing a radio report of King's death.*

"Shortly afterward the report came over the radio that the shooting was fatal. For some reason, that didn't affect me as much as the first attack, when he was stabbed. When he was stabbed, I was shocked at the idea that anyone would try to hurt him. By the time he was assassinated, I had come to realize that there were people who wished him harm. Mama and I wept quietly together."

King's death sparked a wave of riots across America. The violence engulfed more than one hundred cities, causing thirty-nine deaths and millions of dollars in damage.

march through Memphis in honor of her husband. Eight days later, the garbage workers ended their strike when management offered a substantial wage increase.

The Search for James Earl Ray

A massive manhunt turned up vital clues. Witnesses had spotted a man speeding away from the scene in a white Mustang. Near the scene, police located a rifle with a telescopic sight wrapped in a bundle, and fingerprints were found in the room from where the shots had been fired.

Authorities quickly identified the man as James Earl Ray, an escaped convict. For two months Ray successfully eluded police, but he was arrested at London's Heathrow Airport in June and brought back to the United States. At his trial, Ray pled guilty to first-degree murder to avoid receiving the death penalty and was sentenced to ninety-nine years in prison. Three days after sentencing, Ray recanted the confession and asked for a trial, but a judge denied his request.

Because no trial took place to settle questions, a continuing controversy exists about why Ray shot King and whether he acted alone. Some even go as far as to question his involvement in the assassination,

The FBI issued this flyer when they connected escaped prisoner James Earl Ray to Martin Luther King's murder.

asserting that the FBI or an international conspiracy linked to John Kennedy's death played a part. Ray claimed that an underworld figure, mysteriously named Raoul, set him up to take the blame, but no evidence has ever been found that this person exists.

Coretta King, eager to put the issue to rest, called for a trial in 1997. Though no trial was granted, Memphis prosecutors reopened the investigation and concluded that Ray acted alone. The issue became moot when Ray died of liver disease on April 23, 1998.

King Is Laid to Rest

Coretta and A. D. King brought King's body home to Atlanta in a jet chartered by Robert Kennedy. On April 9 almost one hundred thousand mourners gathered outside Ebenezer Baptist Church to hear over loudspeakers Abernathy officiate at King's funeral. During the ceremony a tape of King's final sermon at Ebenezer was played. In that talk he mentioned what he would like done at his funeral. "I don't want a long speech. I'd like somebody to mention that day that Martin Luther King, Jr., tried to give his life for others. I'd like somebody to say that day that Martin Luther King, Jr., tried to love somebody." [130]

After the service pallbearers placed King's body on a hearse that typified the man and his work on behalf of the downtrodden—a simple farm cart pulled by two mules. As the cart wound through Atlanta toward Morehouse College, a lengthy procession of famous individuals, including diplomats, politicians, actors, athletes, and civil rights activists, mixed with the average citizens whose lives King worked so hard to affect. One portion of the route wound directly by Georgia's capitol, which housed the avowed segregationist Governor Lester Maddox, who had objected to closing state schools or lowering flags to half-mast in honor of King.

At Morehouse, King's former professor, Dr. Benjamin Mays, eulogized his slain student:

> God called the grandson of a slave on his father's side, and said to him: Martin Luther, speak to America about war and peace; about social justice and racial discrimination; about its obligations to the poor; and about nonviolence as a way of perfecting social change in a world of brutality and war.[131]

Mays added that many renowned individuals had died young, as did King, including Jesus of Nazareth, Joan of Arc, and John F. Kennedy, but "it isn't how long but how well"[132] one lived.

King's body was then taken to South View Cemetery, where King was buried near his Grandmother Williams. Inscribed on his

Plow mules draw the wagon bearing the casket of Martin Luther King Jr. along the funeral procession route in his hometown of Atlanta on April 9, 1968.

King's final resting place in Atlanta.

crypt were the words he made so famous: "FREE AT LAST, FREE AT LAST, THANK GOD ALMIGHTY I'M FREE AT LAST."

King's Legacy

During his extraordinary lifetime King certainly helped improve people's lives. He saw wrong and, instead of remaining in the background as many do, he took action to correct the injustices. As Jesse Jackson states, King "didn't just talk brotherhood; he was a brother. He didn't just talk friendship; he was a friend. He didn't just talk change; he was a change agent. He didn't wish for change; he

changed things."[133] King illustrated that problems, no matter how large, can be solved through peaceful means if one is willing to strive with every ounce of effort.

His influence, however, extends far beyond his tragic death. Thirty years later in Detroit, Michigan, a group of young adults formed an organization called KOPS—Kids, Organizations, Parents, and Schools. Their goal is to use King's nonviolent means to prevent school problems from escalating out of control. One of the workers, nineteen-year-old Mario Dewberry, says that while he knew about Martin Luther King Jr., it was not until his work with KOPS that he understood King's full impact. Dewberry claims that "studying his principles and his life really

King's Influence

Perhaps no words summarize King's influence better than those of Robert Kennedy during a visit to South Africa. Joy Hakim includes the quote in her book All the People.

"Each time a man stands up for an ideal, or acts to improve the lot of others, or strikes out against injustice, he sends a tiny ripple of hope, and crossing each other from a million different centers of energy and daring, these ripples will build a current which can sweep down the mightiest walls of oppression and resistance."

A mourner breaks down and is consoled by another mourner at the funeral of Martin Luther King. Even after his death, King's dream of racial harmony, equality, and justice lives on.

made me sit back and think about how much of a courageous person he was. He really had to be courageous to put himself on the line like that and never fight back with violence." [134]

King's legacy thus affects youth even today. However, his impact is possibly best expressed by an eighty-nine-year-old black man from Atlanta, Virge Parker:

When I was young, the Ku Klux Klan hung a boy 'cause a white girl say he looked at her. Driving down to Florida one time, a man refused to sell me gas. Just 'cause I was black. But Dr. King, he changed a lot of things. He said there'll come a time when white chillun and black chillun will play together. That happened. And all the folks down at city hall, they all black folks. I'm sure glad I lived long enough to see things turn out the way they did. All those bad old days, they gone with the wind. [135]

Notes

Introduction: A Fighter till the End

1. Quoted in James Melvin Washington, ed., *A Testament of Hope: The Essential Writings and Speeches of Martin Luther King Jr.* New York: Harper & Row, 1986, p. 420.

2. Quoted in Washington, *A Testament of Hope*, p. 420.

3. Quoted in Washington, *A Testament of Hope*, p. 420.

4. Quoted in Stephen B. Oates, *Let the Trumpet Sound: A Life of Martin Luther King Jr.* New York: HarperPerennial, 1994, p. 9.

5. Quoted in Oates, *Let the Trumpet Sound*, p. 404.

6. Quoted in Oates, *Let the Trumpet Sound*, p. 283.

7. Quoted in Flip Schulke and Penelope McPhee, *King Remembered.* New York: Pocket Books, 1986, p. 274.

Chapter 1: "The Curtain Had Dropped on My Selfhood"

8. Quoted in Oates, *Let the Trumpet Sound*, p. 5.

9. Quoted in Oates, *Let the Trumpet Sound*, p. 15.

10. Quoted in Stephen J. Whitfield, *A Death in the Delta: The Story of Emmett Till.* Baltimore: Johns Hopkins University Press, 1988, p. 8.

11. Melba Pattillo Beals, *Warriors Don't Cry.* New York: Pocket Books, 1994, p. 6.

12. Quoted in Washington, *A Testament of Hope*, p. 421.

13. Quoted in Oates, *Let the Trumpet Sound*, p. 10.

14. Quoted in Washington, *A Testament of Hope*, pp. 420–421.

15. Quoted in Washington, *A Testament of Hope*, p. 421.

16. Quoted in Oates, *Let the Trumpet Sound*, p. 12.

17. Quoted in Washington, *A Testament of Hope*, p. 343.

18. Quoted in Oates, *Let the Trumpet Sound*, p. 17.

19. Quoted in Oates, *Let the Trumpet Sound*, p. 17.

Chapter 2: "A Moral Obligation to Return"

20. Quoted in Schulke and McPhee, *King Remembered*, p. 14.

21. Quoted in Oates, *Let the Trumpet Sound*, p. 21.

22. Quoted in Jules Archer, *They Had a Dream.* New York: Puffin Books, 1993, p. 127.

23. Quoted in Schulke and McPhee, *King Remembered*, p. 20.

24. Quoted in Oates, *Let the Trumpet Sound*, p. 43.

25. Quoted in Oates, *Let the Trumpet Sound*, p. 45.

26. Quoted in Oates, *Let the Trumpet Sound*, p. 48.

Chapter 3: "Why Do You Push Us Around?"

27. Quoted in Oates, *Let the Trumpet Sound*, p. 57.

28. Quoted in Schulke and McPhee, *King Remembered*, p. 35.

29. Quoted in Oates, *Let the Trumpet Sound*, p. 64.

30. Quoted in Washington, *A Testament of Hope*, p. 425.

31. Quoted in Oates, *Let the Trumpet Sound*, p. 67.

32. Quoted in Washington, *A Testament of Hope*, p. 430.

33. Quoted in Oates, *Let the Trumpet Sound*, p. 68.

34. Quoted in Oates, *Let the Trumpet Sound*, pp. 70–71.

35. Quoted in Oates, *Let the Trumpet Sound*, p. 72.

36. Quoted in Oates, *Let the Trumpet Sound*, pp. 73, 76–77.

37. Quoted in Oates, *Let the Trumpet Sound*, p. 78.

38. Quoted in Oates, *Let the Trumpet Sound*, p. 80.

39. Quoted in Oates, *Let the Trumpet Sound*, p. 87.

40. Quoted in Oates, *Let the Trumpet Sound*, p. 88.

41. Quoted in Oates, *Let the Trumpet Sound*, p. 89.

42. Quoted in Oates, *Let the Trumpet Sound*, p. 90.

43. Quoted in Oates, *Let the Trumpet Sound*, p. 93.

44. Quoted in Oates, *Let the Trumpet Sound*, p. 93.

45. Quoted in Washington, *A Testament of Hope*, pp. 455–56.

46. Quoted in Oates, *Let the Trumpet Sound*, pp. 103–104.

47. Quoted in Washington, *A Testament of Hope*, p. 462.

48. Quoted in Schulke and McPhee, *King Remembered*, p. 60.

49. Quoted in Oates, *Let the Trumpet Sound*, p. 112.

50. Quoted in Schulke and McPhee, *King Remembered*, p. 69.

Chapter 4: "Injustice Anywhere Is a Threat"

51. Quoted in Oates, *Let the Trumpet Sound*, p. 118.

52. Quoted in Schulke and McPhee, *King Remembered*, p. 70.

53. Quoted in Schulke and McPhee, *King Remembered*, p. 70.

54. Quoted in Oates, *Let the Trumpet Sound*, p. 127.

55. Quoted in Oates, *Let the Trumpet Sound*, p. 139.

56. Quoted in Oates, *Let the Trumpet Sound*, p. 139.

57. Quoted in Schulke and McPhee, *King Remembered*, p. 90.

58. Quoted in Schulke and McPhee, *King Remembered*, p. 83.

59. Quoted in Schulke and McPhee, *King Remembered*, p. 79.

60. Quoted in Washington, *A Testament of Hope*, p. 407.

61. Quoted in Schulke and McPhee, *King Remembered*, p. 94.

62. Quoted in Oates, *Let the Trumpet Sound*, p. 165.

63. Quoted in Oates, *Let the Trumpet Sound*, p. 175.

64. Quoted in Oates, *Let the Trumpet Sound*, pp. 176–77.

65. Quoted in Taylor Branch, *Parting the Waters: America in the King Years, 1954–1963*. New York: Simon & Schuster, 1988, p. 557.

66. Quoted in Washington, *A Testament of Hope*, p. 342.

67. Quoted in Oates, *Let the Trumpet Sound*, p. 198.

Chapter 5: "'Wait' Has Almost Always Meant 'Never'"

68. Quoted in Oates, *Let the Trumpet Sound*, p. 206.

69. Quoted in Washington, *A Testament of Hope*, p. 523.

70. Quoted in Oates, *Let the Trumpet Sound*, p. 210.

71. Quoted in Oates, *Let the Trumpet Sound*, p. 212.

72. Quoted in Archer, *They Had a Dream*, p. 153.

73. Quoted in Schulke and McPhee, *King Remembered*, p. 123.

74. Quoted in Branch, *Parting the Waters*, pp. 737–38.

75. Martin Luther King Jr., *"Letter from Birmingham Jail" and "I Have a Dream" Speech*. Logan, IA: Perfection Learning, 1990, pp. 3, 9–12, 18, 37.

76. Quoted in Branch, *Parting the Waters*, p. 759.

77. Quoted in Branch, *Parting the Waters*, p. 762.

78. Quoted in Washington, *A Testament of Hope*, p. 540.

79. Quoted in Washington, *A Testament of Hope*, pp. 546–47.

80. Quoted in Washington, *A Testament of Hope*, p. 376.

81. Quoted in Washington, *A Testament of Hope*, p. 347.

82. Quoted in Arthur M. Schlesinger Jr., *A Thousand Days: John F. Kennedy in the White House*. Boston: Houghton Mifflin, 1965, p. 965.

83. Quoted in Washington, *A Testament of Hope*, p. 528.

84. Quoted in Schulke and McPhee, *King Remembered*, p. 132.

85. Quoted in Oates, *Let the Trumpet Sound*, p. 253.

Chapter 6: "Let Freedom Ring"

86. Quoted in Schulke and McPhee, *King Remembered*, p. 154.

87. King, *"Letter from Birmingham Jail" and "I Have a Dream" Speech*, pp. 38, 42–46.

88. Quoted in Schulke and McPhee, *King Remembered*, p. 157.

89. Quoted in Oates, *Let the Trumpet Sound*, p. 270.

90. Quoted in Washington, *A Testament of Hope*, pp. 355–56.

91. Quoted in Oates, *Let the Trumpet Sound*, p. 301.

92. Quoted in Washington, *A Testament of Hope*, p. 351.

93. Quoted in Oates, *Let the Trumpet Sound*, p. 299.

94. Quoted in Oates, *Let the Trumpet Sound*, p. 301.

95. Quoted in Oates, *Let the Trumpet Sound*, p. 301.

96. Quoted in Schulke and McPhee, *King Remembered*, p. 177.

97. Quoted in Gary M. Pomerantz, *Where Peachtree Meets Sweet Auburn*. New York: Scribner, 1996, p. 335.

98. Quoted in Schulke and McPhee, *King Remembered*, pp. 177–79.

99. Quoted in Oates, *Let the Trumpet Sound*, p. 331.

100. Quoted in Oates, *Let the Trumpet Sound*, p. 334.

Chapter 7: "I Wept Within That Night"

101. Quoted in Schulke and McPhee, *King Remembered*, p. 182.

102. Quoted in Oates, *Let the Trumpet Sound*, p. 341.

103. Quoted in Schulke and McPhee, *King Remembered*, pp. 192–93.

104. Quoted in Schulke and McPhee, *King Remembered*, p. 194.

105. Quoted in Washington, *A Testament of Hope*, pp. 581–82.

106. Quoted in Schulke and McPhee, *King Remembered*, p. 209.

107. Quoted in Washington, *A Testament of Hope*, p. 353.

108. Quoted in Washington, *A Testament of Hope*, p. 595.

109. Quoted in Washington, *A Testament of Hope*, p. 591.

110. Quoted in Oates, *Let the Trumpet Sound*, p. 377.

111. Quoted in Oates, *Let the Trumpet Sound*, p. 413.

112. Quoted in Oates, *Let the Trumpet Sound*, p. 413.

113. Quoted in Schulke and McPhee, *King Remembered*, p. 234.

114. Quoted in Washington, *A Testament of Hope*, p. 404.

115. Quoted in Oates, *Let the Trumpet Sound*, p. 397.

Chapter 8: "Free at Last"

116. Quoted in Washington, *A Testament of Hope*, p. 490.

117. Quoted in Oates, *Let the Trumpet Sound*, pp. 434–36.

118. Quoted in Oates, *Let the Trumpet Sound*, p. 455.

119. Quoted in Oates, *Let the Trumpet Sound*, p. 465.

120. Quoted in Oates, *Let the Trumpet Sound*, pp. 482–83.

121. Quoted in Schulke and McPhee, *King Remembered*, p. 245.

122. Quoted in Schulke and McPhee, *King Remembered*, p. 245.

123. Quoted in Oates, *Let the Trumpet Sound*, pp. 490–91.

124. Quoted in Pomerantz, *Where Peachtree Meets Sweet Auburn*, p. 355.

125. Quoted in Schulke and McPhee, *King Remembered*, p. 250.

126. Quoted in Oates, *Let the Trumpet Sound*, p. 493.

127. Quoted in Schulke and McPhee, *King Remembered*, p. 250.

128. Quoted in Oates, *Let the Trumpet Sound*, p. 494.

129. Quoted in Schulke and McPhee, *King Remembered*, pp. 251, 254.

130. Quoted in Schulke and McPhee, *King Remembered*, p. 262.

131. Quoted in Oates, *Let the Trumpet Sound*, p. 497.

132. Quoted in Pomerantz, *Where Peachtree Meets Sweet Auburn*, p. 362.

133. Quoted in Schulke and McPhee, *King Remembered*, p. 274.

134. Quoted in Cassandra Spratling, "Living the Dream," *Detroit Free Press*, April 3, 1998, p. 2F.

135. Quoted in Schulke and McPhee, *King Remembered*, pp. 273–74.

For Further Reading

David A. Adler, *Martin Luther King Jr.: Free at Last.* New York: Holiday House, 1986. A brief biography for elementary students.

Jim Bishop, *The Days of Martin Luther King Jr.* New York: Putnam, 1971. A readable account of King's life, written by a respected journalist.

James T. DeKay, *Meet Martin Luther King Jr.* New York: Random House, 1993. A useful introduction to King's life, written for the upper elementary level.

Editors of Time-Life Books, *This Fabulous Century: 1960–1970.* New York: Time-Life Books, 1970. An engaging look at the decade in which King carried out many of his most important campaigns.

Kai Frieze, *Rosa Parks: The Movement Organizes.* Englewood Cliffs, NJ: Silver Burdett, 1990. A valuable survey of Parks's life.

Mary Hull, *Rosa Parks.* New York: Chelsea House, 1994. A fine biography of the civil rights pioneer written for the junior high school student.

Robert Jakoubek, *Martin Luther King Jr.* New York: Chelsea House, 1989. Written for the junior high and high school student, this biography provides a balanced look at Martin Luther King Jr.'s life and impact.

Frank B. Latham, *The Rise and Fall of "Jim Crow," 1865–1964.* New York: Franklin Watts, 1969. A useful account of the origins of legal discrimination in the South, written for junior high school students.

George Metcalf, *Black Profiles.* New York: McGraw-Hill, 1968. A helpful summary of the lives of key civil rights leaders.

Michael A. Schuman, *Martin Luther King Jr.: Leader for Civil Rights.* Springfield, NJ: Enslow, 1996. A good biography for junior high school students.

Dorothy Sterling, *Tear Down the Walls!: A History of the American Civil Rights Movement.* Garden City, NY: Doubleday, 1968. Contains some helpful information on Jim Crow laws and other aspects of civil rights.

Works Consulted

Jules Archer, *They Had a Dream*. New York: Puffin Books, 1993. An excellent account of the civil rights struggle that focuses on four individuals, including King.

Melba Pattillo Beals, *Warriors Don't Cry*. New York: Pocket Books, 1994. A gripping account of the first year at Little Rock's integrated Central High School, written by one of the participants.

Taylor Branch, *Parting the Waters: America in the King Years, 1954–1963*. New York: Simon & Schuster, 1988. The definitive story of King's role in the civil rights movement.

"Confessed King Killer Dies at 70," *Detroit Free Press,* April 24, 1998. A brief newspaper article about the death of James Earl Ray.

Adam Fairclough, *Martin Luther King Jr.* Athens: University of Georgia Press, 1995. A helpful biography of King written in scholarly fashion.

John Hope Franklin, *From Slavery to Freedom: A History of Negro Americans*. New York: Knopf, 1974. Written by one of the nation's foremost historians, this book provides useful information on the history of African Americans.

Joy Hakim, *All the People*. New York: Oxford University Press, 1995. A readable history of the modern-day United States, including King and civil rights, written for the junior high school student.

Martin Luther King Jr., *"Letter from Birmingham Jail" and "I Have a Dream" Speech*. Logan, IA: Perfection Learning, 1990. A reprint of King's two most famous documents, which should be required reading for every teenager. The beauty and power of King's words are inspiring.

———, *The Strength to Love*. New York: Harper & Row, 1963. An enlightening collection of many of King's sermons.

———, *Stride Toward Freedom: The Montgomery Story*. New York: Harper & Brothers, 1958. King's account of the momentous bus boycott.

———, *The Trumpet of Conscience*. New York: Harper & Row, 1968. A second collection of King's sermons, which includes his anti–Vietnam War statements.

———, *Where Do We Go from Here: Chaos or Community?* New York: Harper & Row, 1967. King's heartfelt plea for cooperation in the civil rights movement, written as the advocacy of violence by some black leaders became more prevalent.

———, *Why We Can't Wait*. New York: New American Library, 1964. King's defense of nonviolence that contains much helpful information on his Birmingham and other southern campaigns.

Walter Dean Myers, *Malcolm X: By Any Means Necessary*. New York: Scholastic, 1993. Outstanding biography of the civil rights leader.

Stephen B. Oates, *Let the Trumpet Sound: A Life of Martin Luther King Jr.* New York: HarperPerennial, 1994. An award-winning biography written in a compelling style, this book is essential for an understanding of the subject.

Rosa Parks, with Jim Haskins, *Rosa Parks: My Story.* New York: Scholastic, 1992. The autobiography of the woman who started the Montgomery bus boycott, intended for the teenage market.

Gary M. Pomerantz, *Where Peachtree Meets Sweet Auburn.* New York: Scribner, 1996. Fine narrative of Atlanta's growth that focuses on the issue of civil rights.

Arthur M. Schlesinger Jr., *A Thousand Days: John F. Kennedy in the White House.* Boston: Houghton Mifflin, 1965. An excellent account of President Kennedy's brief tenure that contains useful material on his dealings with King.

Flip Schulke and Penelope McPhee, *King Remembered.* New York: Pocket Books, 1986. A valuable account of King's life based on the recollections of his coworkers, friends, and family.

Cassandra Spratling, "Living the Dream," *Detroit Free Press*, April 3, 1998. An article featuring the work of Detroit-area youths who employ nonviolence to resolve disputes among students.

James Melvin Washington, ed., *A Testament of Hope: The Essential Writings and Speeches of Martin Luther King Jr.* New York: Harper & Row, 1986. An indispensable compilation of King's writings, speeches, and interviews that contains practically every public utterance issued by Martin Luther King Jr.

Stephen J. Whitfield, *A Death in the Delta: The Story of Emmett Till.* Baltimore: Johns Hopkins University Press, 1988. The moving story of the shocking murder of Emmett Till. It also contains illuminating information about being black in the South in the early 1900s.

Index

Picture Credits

About the Author

John F. Wukovits is a junior high school teacher and writer from Trenton, Michigan, who specializes in history and biography. Besides a biography of Anne Frank for Lucent, he has written biographies of Admiral Clifton Sprague, Barry Sanders, Tim Allen, Jack Nicklaus, Vince Lombardi, and Wyatt Earp. A graduate of the University of Notre Dame, Wukovits is the father of three daughters—Amy, Julie, and Karen.